RED-HANDED

RED-HANDED

CONDUCTING SMARTER
WORKERS' COMPENSATION INVESTIGATIONS
TO REDUCE FRAUD AND CLAIMS COST

JR ROBLES

LIONCREST
PUBLISHING

RED-HANDED

Conducting Smarter Workers' Compensation
Investigations to Reduce Fraud and Claims Cost

ISBN   978-1-5445-1123-8 *Paperback*

978-1-5445-1122-1 *Ebook*

Dedicated to my mom and dad. It's impossible to thank you adequately for everything you've done, from loving me unconditionally, teaching me the value of hard work, and encouraging me to dream big.

CONTENTS

INTRODUCTION

Juan was a twenty-nine-year-old dishwasher. His duties included grabbing dishes from the rack, bringing them to his station, stacking them three high, rinsing them, scrubbing them, putting them in a tub, and then placing them into the dishwasher. One month after quitting his job, he filed an insurance claim, alleging that he'd sustained injuries to his left knee and lower back during a fall while employed at the restaurant.

Due to the injuries, he now required medical treatment. This is known as a post-termination claim. It's extremely common—and it's a huge, red flag. By the time the employer became aware of the claim, Juan had already retained a lawyer, and a month had passed, which meant some vital evidence was gone. For example, the video cameras that would have captured the incident had been taped over. Also, some of the witnesses who worked there at the same time had moved on to other places without providing forwarding addresses or phone numbers. Those who could be contacted found their memories of that time period had faded.

These factors put the employer at a distinct disadvantage. Fortunately, in a case like this, the employer has ninety days to review the claim, which allows for a reasonable but expeditious investigation into the merits of the claim.

Since Juan never reported the injury to his employer while on the job, he didn't receive the proper paperwork to file for workers' compensation, and he didn't obtain medical care. That means the employer and their insurance provider lost the opportunity to choose a doctor. Instead, he went out and found a doctor on his own. That doctor, an orthopedist named Dr. Johnson, happens to be quite favorable to injured workers, because she has a great relationship with the lawyer that Juan retained.

Dr. Johnson claimed Juan could no longer work and needed a lot of serious medical care, so she went ahead with treatment procedures. The restaurant's insurance company had seen enough red flags, so they denied the claim and launched an investigation. Since the claim was now denied, Dr. Johnson also filed a lien to recover payment for services rendered.

Daniel, the executive chef and Juan's direct supervisor, said that after Juan quit, he decided a few weeks later he wanted his job back. The chef turned him down, and Juan filed the post-termination claim almost immediately afterward. The chef also said that Juan never reported any injury, pain, or soreness while employed. As a matter of fact, he had never shown any physical symptoms at all or said anything on the subject. On the contrary, he'd been a very fast and efficient worker.

Other employees also said Juan's injury was news to them. They pointed out that he'd previously gotten hurt riding a motorcycle, an accident that happened while he was employed by the restaurant. Also, he had an ongoing personal injury lawsuit stemming from an earlier traffic accident in which a car driven by an elderly woman struck him while he was riding a bicycle. He'd missed numerous days of work in order to go to court. Further investigation confirmed both of these incidents.

Shortly before his alleged workplace accident, Juan received a cash settlement from his traffic accident case, and he shared some of that money with his work buddies. An employee named Alex said he was offered $500 by Juan to say he witnessed the injury at the restaurant.

Curiously, the traffic accident resulted in injuries to Juan's left knee and lower back, and the same lawyer who represented him in that case was now representing him in his workers' compensation claim against his former employer. In his deposition and on all of his claims forms, Juan asserted that he'd never had any prior injuries.

The employer's insurance company subpoenaed the doctors involved in the first case to testify against Juan. The doctors explained the medical procedures they'd performed in treating him, including surgery. Dr. Johnson told the court that Juan had never mentioned any of those treatment procedures.

With more red flags appearing, the insurance company initiated a more thorough investigation, including surveillance. The executive chef provided helpful advice to the investigation, explaining that Juan was a gym rat, lifting weights two or three times a day and taking boxing classes every week. Juan told the doctor that ever since the accident, he couldn't bend, lift, or even stoop down. He could only be on his feet for about ten minutes at a time. However, during surveillance, Juan was spotted bounding out of the doctor's office, a spring in his step. He climbed on his motorcycle and headed to the gym, where he was observed doing 400-pound leg presses. Later in the day, he visited a second gym for boxing lessons, hopping around the ring with no sign of pain.

Ultimately, Juan was charged and convicted of workers'

compensation insurance fraud in San Diego County and ordered to pay more than $20,000 in restitution fees.

The insurance company incurred expenses in filing and managing the claim. The investigation cost $8,000. By nine months into the case, Juan's medical care, including prescription painkillers, physical therapy, and follow-up visits, had added up. The insurance company stopped the bleeding a little bit by denying payment to Juan's doctor. Had the insurance company not investigated the claim, however, they would've been on the hook for untold thousands of dollars in medical expenses. They also would've been responsible for his workers' compensation temporary disability benefits, which amounted to two-thirds of his regular salary and could've lasted up to two years. On top of that, they would have paid long-term disability or retraining costs, since Juan allegedly couldn't go back to work as a dishwasher.

All of these costs, along with legal fees, meant the insurance company could have been looking at tens of thousands of dollars.

THE PROBLEM

No matter your role with respect to insurance claims—claims manager, claims supervisor, risk manager, VP of claims, claims examiner, human resources, or an attorney representing any of the above—you probably already have a working knowledge of investigations and some idea of their benefit. Everyone in the industry acknowledges their necessity as a fraud prevention measure. Whatever business you're in, public or private, you understand that people are going to get hurt, employees and customers alike, and that injuries are par for the course. Some claims will be legitimate, others won't. However, most are going to fall somewhere in between, and this book is designed to address those cases.

The ever-changing legal landscape is a minefield for companies and the managers tasked with handling their insurance claims, whether they manage their own claims department, use a third-party administrator, or have an insurance company that insures and manages claims on their behalf.

IN-HOUSE INSURANCE

Many large companies choose to self-insure. Pepsi, Macy's, and Walmart, for example, don't buy insurance from Liberty Mutual, or Traveler's, or Progressive; they pay claims directly from their profits. Any claim that can be reduced, whether it's a legal defense, a medical defense, or an investigation, helps their bottom line. Because claims come in constantly, a company like Walmart needs to reserve $500 million to $1 billion in a given year to pay for claims, administer benefits, and defend themselves. So if they can use investigators, lawyers, and doctors to reduce that cost, it's a victory.[1]

The reason large companies prefer to self-insure is because insurance is a business. It has a profit margin. Companies that have the necessary cash want to avoid contributing those profits to an insurance company by running their own in-house insurance operation at cost.

Walmart has roughly 1.8 million employees in the United States. Many of those jobs involve lifting and moving boxes. It's physical work, so the company receives many claims. They also have billions of dollars in profits, so they have the money to self-insure and an incentive to fight fraud, since they can't simply pass the cost along to anyone other than their own customers.

It's easy to see why companies who self-insure are motivated to prevent paying fraudulent or exaggerated claims—that money comes directly out of the till. For public agencies, it's especially important because fraudulent claims can impact budgets, reducing services like fire, safety, police, and social programs. Being self-insured also gives the employer the ability to control claims more efficiently than with a carrier or third-party administrator

---

1   U.S. Courts. "Litigation Cost Survey of Major Companies." http://www.uscourts.gov/sites/default/files/litigation_cost_survey_of_major_companies_0.pdf (retrieved May 8, 2018).

(TPA), since they only focus on their own claims and not those of other employers.

OUTSIDE INSURANCE

Some companies buy insurance on the market. Even though they aren't paying claims out of pocket, they still have a vested interest in trying to reduce the cost of those claims in a variety of ways—medical, legal, investigations—because, like a self-insured company, they want to reduce total costs. Those costs ultimately affect their rates for the following year. All employers have what's known as an "experience modification rate" (XMOD), which we can understand with this simple formula:

$$Experience\ Modification\ Rate = Actual\ Losses/Expected\ Losses$$

The XMOD either rewards or penalizes companies with lower or higher claims and claims management. The Workers' Compensation Insurance Rating Bureau of California (WCIRB) calculates XMOD ratings.

Let's look at two hypothetical roofing companies to understand how this might look in practice. Company A has a hundred employees and has never had a workers' compensation claim. Their premiums per employee are 30 percent of their salary, so for a $10-per-hour worker, they pay $3 for workers' compensation insurance.

Company B has had three claims, and they've been significant—major back injuries, orthopedic claims, and psychological claims, resulting in huge settlements, and keeping people off work on temporary disability benefits (TTD) for lengthy amounts of time. As a result, their workers' comp premium is 50 percent of their salary, so they're paying fifty cents on the dollar, or $15 per hour for the same potential worker.

When the two roofing companies bid on a new school in the city, Company B simply can't compete, because their labor cost has gone way up due to workers' comp.

THIRD-PARTY ADMINISTRATORS

For both self-insured employers and those who use outside insurance companies, there's another resource: third-party administrators (TPAs). It makes sense for a self-insured company to hire a TPA to handle their claims, but even a company that is insured by a carrier might request that a TPA handle their claims. This can provide a greater degree of confidence that claims will be handled effectively.

A TPA focuses on administering benefits in accordance with state laws for a separate entity, like a pool of self-insured employers, self-insured public entities, or even insurance companies that outsource their claims administration.

A GUIDE FOR CLAIMS EXAMINERS

The frontline claims examiner's job is to administer claims benefits, not to deprive anyone of benefits, but to adjudicate claims impartially, professionally, and as quickly as possible. They make sure the person filing the claim receives the medical treatment they need by authorizing the bills for treatment. That might mean finding a lawyer, or securing an in-home nurse, acquiring reliable transportation, or paying for a wheelchair.

If something appears suspicious, the claims examiner might have to hire an investigator, since they are required by law to investigate and submit reports to the state in suspected cases of fraud. If the injured worker gets a lawyer, the claims examiner hires the lawyer. If bills coming in from the doctor seem high, the claims examiner may send the medical bills to a bill review company.

Claims examiners are the quarterbacks of the claim; they make many decisions on the administration of many issues—legal, medical, investigations, language, transportation—so they don't have enough time in the day to be an expert in all of those fields. What they do have is a great deal of autonomy to make decisions on who they use and when they use them, ensuring best practices.

Ideally, this book will serve as a guide for claims examiners, helping them work faster and more efficiently by using investigative resources for maximum gain.

SHINING A LIGHT INTO GRAY AREAS

By getting an investigation started early, you can shape the direction of the claim itself and avoid spending unnecessary money early on, because early detection saves money.

As investigators, we shine a light into gray areas. We corroborate legitimate claims, expose fraudulent ones, and examine everything in between. We determine if a claim is accurate by conducting investigations, including background checks, criminal history, and prior medical claims, to learn if an injured worker has ever had similar injuries or past lawsuits.

We stay current with applicable laws governing privacy because they're ever changing. New technologies constantly redraw the boundaries of privacy, and because of the speed of today's technology, those boundaries are shifting more rapidly than ever before. New cases get filed faster than the courts can keep up. Precedents are set one day and overturned the next, with no definitive guidelines established.

Keeping abreast of the parameters of privacy has become a full-time job, and many investigators don't know where the lines are in terms of social media, drones, infrared cameras, or GPS trackers with regard to surveillance. This legal uncertainty creates a problem for companies who might try to use investigative measures as a tool against fraud.

In the following pages, we'll dive into the legal and practical aspects of investigations, with an eye toward best practices, drawing on the most recent case law and statutes. We'll also discuss tips for conducting online investigations.

My goal is to help you better understand the tools at your disposal, when to deploy them, and what your expectations should be. In the end, you'll have a much better understanding of where investigators fit into the puzzle and what you can do in the scope of your own investigations. By understanding how to conduct effective investigations, you'll avoid or expose fraud and save money.

CHAPTER 1

THE ELEMENTS OF FRAUD

Twenty-nine-year-old Joe had been on the job fewer than ninety days when he got hurt, so he was still in his probationary period. Although every employer varies in regard to their probationary period, in Joe's case it meant he didn't yet have health coverage. While playing softball on a Saturday two days earlier, he tore a tendon in his knee sliding into third base. It wasn't a work-related injury. It wasn't even the company team.

Because he didn't have health insurance, he didn't go to urgent care. Instead, he returned to work Monday morning, clocked in, got his delivery sheet manifests, loaded up his truck, and drove off. About an hour later, he called his boss saying he had hurt his knee while lifting a heavy package. There were no witnesses.

The company sent out another driver to cover the route, and they took Joe to urgent care. Sure enough, his knee was torn up and needed surgery, so the company immediately began the claims process.

The claims examiner knew there was nothing inherently suspicious about a delivery driver getting hurt lifting a heavy package. Still, Joe was a new employee, and nobody had witnessed the injury. If these aren't exactly red flags, they're certainly yellow flags. Just to be thorough, the claims examiner decided it was worth looking into further, so they referred the claim to us for investigation.

The first thing any investigator does is a background check. After completion of an initial criminal and civil background check, we found nothing either derogatory or helpful to the claim.

The next step was a social media search. In doing so, we found out the injured worker played on a softball team. We obtained the schedule and learned he had been in attendance on the previous Saturday. During additional research, we didn't find any videos of the game on YouTube.

Joe's Facebook profile was blocked to the public, but the

softball team had its own public page. We looked at that page and found other players with open profiles. On their pages, we saw messages to Joe that said things like, "Hey, Joe, tough break at the game. Hope your leg gets better soon." We even saw pictures of Joe at that very game. It was clear Joe had injured himself at the softball game the Saturday before the claim was filed.

During the AOE/COE (Arising Out of Employment/ Course of Employment) portion of the investigation, we asked directly if he had been injured at any time before that Monday morning when he made the claim. He said no. We asked him if he played any sports. He said he occasionally played softball, but he didn't say anything about playing recently. He denied being at the game on Saturday, and, in fact, claimed he hadn't played during the whole season. We didn't reveal that we knew otherwise.

Next, we obtained the medical reports. Joe had also lied to the doctors about the injury. We reported back to the claims examiner and Special Investigation Unit (SIU) director within the TPA, and they denied the claim. However, Joe had already undergone surgery and wanted to make sure the company was going to pay for it. He couldn't go back to work. The injury was legitimate, even if it wasn't work related, so he hired a workers' compensation lawyer in an attempt to fight the denial.

We produced witnesses—teammates and players from the other team—who testified under oath that Joe had hurt his knee during the game. At that point, Joe was cornered. He tried to say the knee injury he'd sustained on Saturday was minor, and that he had suffered the actual tendon damage on Monday.

An independent doctor was brought in, and after he examined Joe's knee, the doctor determined the injury was consistent with an injury one might sustain playing softball and not an injury caused by lifting. The employer prevailed and TPA requested that we refer this claim to the district attorney and Department of Insurance for fraud referral. Joe was convicted and ordered to pay restitution, which included the initial medical bills, the claims administration costs, and the cost of the investigation.

THE MOST PRACTICED FRAUD IN THE WORLD

The insurance business is highly susceptible to fraud, and, as a result, it has become the most widely practiced form of fraud in the world. Since insurance companies generate such a large cash flow, they create an economic resource that is an attractive target. Fraud occurs when individuals attempt to profit in some way from an insurance company without complying with the terms of an insurance agreement. It can happen at any point during an insurance transaction, and it can be perpetrated by individuals applying for insurance, policyholders, third-party claimants, or professionals who provide services to claimants.

Insurance fraud comes in two forms. "Hard fraud" occurs when an accident, injury, or theft of property is fabricated. "Soft fraud" occurs when a legitimate claim is exaggerated.

There are three common types of workers' compensation claimant fraud:

- False Claims. The injury never occurred in the first place and the applicant knowingly made misrepresentations in order to receive benefits.
- Double Dipping. They work while collecting temporary disability payments or other benefits.
- Exaggerated Claims. Workers initially sustain a legitimate injury but then exaggerate the severity or use "injury creep" to collect more money and stay off the job for a longer period of time.

THE RECIPE FOR FRAUD

In 1953, American criminologist Donald Cressey developed a theory known as the Fraud Triangle. According to Cressey, three ingredients will be present in any fraud case: *need*, *opportunity*, and *apathy*. This is the unholy trinity of fraud. When each of these conditions has been met, the possibility of fraud exists. In 2004, David Wolfe and Dana Hermanson in *The CPA Journal* expanded Cressy's Fraud Triangle theory with their own Fraud Diamond Theory. In it, they added *capability* as a new element of fraud. Their theory suggests a fraudster must have both a particular fraud opportunity and the ability to turn it into reality. Capability includes things like position, intelligence, ego, coercion, and deceit.

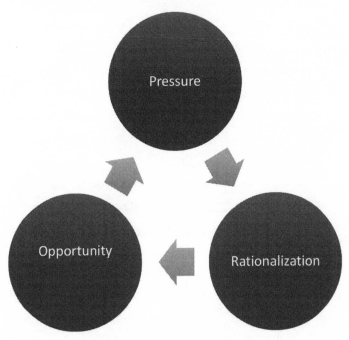

Cressey's Fraud Triangle Theory

Wolfe and Hermanson's Fraud Diamond Theory

Most crimes boil down to *need* or *pressure* in one way or another. Usually, if someone steals a diamond ring, it isn't because that person wants a diamond ring; it's because they need the cash. In the previous illustration, Joe acquired a need when he injured himself. He needed someone to pay his medical bills since he didn't have healthcare for his nonindustrial injury.

Opportunity is the point in the recipe where fraud occurs. Need and apathy are prerequisites, but when the opportunity arises, all the elements necessary for fraud fall into place. In workers' comp cases, the opportunity might come in the form of an environment that lacks supervision or video cameras. It could also be a favorable boss or a weak track record of fraud prevention. In Joe's case, the opportunity came two days after his injury, at a job that required lifting and provided the ability to work unobserved and unsupervised.

Apathy (or *rationalization*) is probably the easiest ingredient in the recipe. Apathy is a form of rationalization in which a person justifies a crime. In this case, Joe probably thought that he wasn't really stealing since he was so close to getting his health insurance anyway. After all, who cares about an arbitrary date? Maybe he felt the probationary period was unfair. He was just as likely to be injured in the first ninety days as the last ninety, so why shouldn't the company cover those costs? Maybe he felt, like most people, that insurance companies ought to be there when you need them, no matter the circumstances. Whatever the case, somehow, he came to believe that lying about the cause of his injury was okay.

Global insurance provider Zurich polled more than two thousand customers to see how they reacted in ethical situations where honesty could have potentially raised their insurance rates. One in five people admitted to lying to their insurance company, even though they knew providing false information could render their policies invalid.

WHERE DOES FRAUD HAPPEN?

According to the Coalition Against Insurance Fraud, fraud costs an estimated $80 billion a year across all lines of insurance, of which $7.2 billion is related to workers' comp. According to NICB (National Insurance Crime Bureau), fraud comprises about 10 percent of the property and casualty insurance losses and loss adjustment expenses each year. It also accounts for between 5 and 10 percent of the claims of U.S. and Canadian insurers. For a third of insurers, fraud represents 20 percent of their total claims cost. The difference between 5 percent and 20 percent is largely the difference between insurers who act aggressively in fighting fraud and those who don't.

All told, insurance fraud accounts for 7 percent of the overall U.S. gross domestic product. Despite this, only a small percentage of cases are ever investigated. An even smaller percentage of the perpetrators are convicted of crimes. Claims that go uninvestigated send the message that it's okay to lie, which perpetuates more fraud. Those costs are then written back into the price of insurance premiums and passed on to the customer. Public agencies simply lay off workers, furlough workers, or reduce services.

APPLICANT FRAUD

The cases we've looked at thus far have been examples of applicant or claimant fraud, in which someone lies in their claim. Joe, who lied about the cause of his knee injury, is a typical example of applicant fraud. According to California Insurance Code 1871.4(a)(1), it is unlawful to "make or cause to be made a knowingly false or fraudulent material statement or material representation for the purpose of obtaining or denying any compensation."

In addition to 1871.4 (a)(1), 484(a) of the California Penal Code is often charged with this type of fraud, both of which are felonies.[2]

> 484. (a) Every person who shall feloniously steal, take, carry, lead, or drive away the personal property of another, or who shall fraudulently appropriate property which has been entrusted to him or her, or who shall knowingly and designedly, by any false or fraudulent representation or pretense, defraud any other person of money, labor or real or personal property, or who causes or procures others to report falsely of his or her wealth or mercantile character and by thus imposing upon any person, obtains credit and thereby fraudulently gets or obtains possession of money, or property or obtains the labor or service of another, is guilty of theft. In determining the value of the property obtained, for the purposes of this section, the reasonable and fair market value shall be the test, and in determining

---

2   California Legislative Information. "CHAPTER 5. Larceny [484 - 502.9] ." https://leginfo. legislature.ca.gov/faces/codes_displaySection.xhtml?sectionNum=484.&lawCode=PEN (accessed May 14, 2018)

the value of services received the contract price shall be the test. If there be no contract price, the reasonable and going wage for the service rendered shall govern. For the purposes of this section, any false or fraudulent representation or pretense made shall be treated as continuing, so as to cover any money, property or service received as a result thereof, and the complaint, information or indictment may charge that the crime was committed on any date during the particular period in question. The hiring of any additional employee or employees without advising each of them of every labor claim due and unpaid and every judgment that the employer has been unable to meet shall be prima facie evidence of intent to defraud.

EMPLOYER FRAUD

Employers also commit fraud. Consider, for instance, a family-run construction business in which the owner's relative—a cousin, let's say—is hurt in a non-work-related (aka nonindustrial) injury. The owner might be inclined to call it an on-the-job injury and have the company's insurance cover the costs.

An even more common example involves employee designations. Suppose you own a roofing company with a hundred employees made up of forty roofers, twenty administrative roles, with the rest being roofers' assistants, drivers, a receptionist, and warehouse workers. The costs of insuring a roofer or a receptionist are quite different. It might cost twenty cents on the dollar for every hour of work the receptionist puts in. That means, at $10 an hour, it's going to cost $1.60 per day to cover that employee. The roofer, at $20 an hour, is involved in more dangerous work, which might require fifty cents on the dollar per hour to cover him. That works out to $80 a day in coverage costs. For the other employees, the costs are probably somewhere between those two extremes.

When a roofer gets hurt, the employer might be tempted to misclassify the employee to the insurance company. Maybe she claims the worker was merely an assistant and didn't do any of the dangerous rooftop work. This relatively small lie represents a substantial portion of insurance fraud.

PROVIDER FRAUD

When providers commit fraud, it tends to happen on a larger scale. If a doctor is committing fraud with one patient, he's probably doing it with all of his patients. We investigated an orthopedic surgeon who specialized in knee and hip replacement. He'd order a bunch of unnecessary MRIs, prescribe unnecessary medical devices, and bill insurance providers for visits that never occurred.

Laws limit a medical provider's ability to charge on workers' comp claims, but a doctor might believe his time is worth more than he's allowed to bill. That fact could create both the need and apathy. The opportunity arises when it's time to bill.

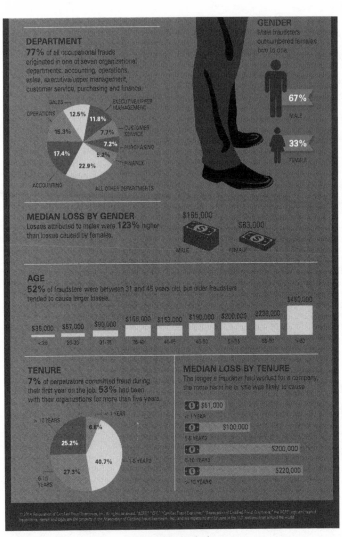

DEPARTMENT

77% of all occupational frauds originated in one of seven organizational departments: accounting, operations, sales, executive/upper management, customer service, purchasing and finance.

- SALES
- OPERATIONS **12.5%**
- **11.8%** EXECUTIVE/UPPER MANAGEMENT
- **15.3%**
- **7.7%** CUSTOMER SERVICE
- **7.2%** PURCHASING
- **17.4%**
- **5.2%** FINANCE
- **22.9%**
- ACCOUNTING
- ALL OTHER DEPARTMENTS

GENDER

Male fraudsters outnumbered females two to one.

67% MALE

33% FEMALE

MEDIAN LOSS BY GENDER

Losses attributed to males were **123%** higher than losses caused by females.

$185,000 MALE

$83,000 FEMALE

AGE

52% of fraudsters were between 31 and 45 years old, but older fraudsters tended to cause larger losses.

| $35,000 | $57,000 | $90,000 | $168,000 | $153,000 | $190,000 | $200,000 | $238,000 | $450,000 |
| <26 | 26-30 | 31-35 | 36-40 | 41-45 | 46-50 | 51-55 | 56-60 | >60 |

TENURE

7% of perpetrators committed fraud during their first year on the job. **53%** had been with their organizations for more than five years.

- > 10 YEARS
- < 1 YEAR **6.8%**
- **25.2%**
- **40.7%** 1-5 YEARS
- **27.3%**
- 6-10 YEARS

MEDIAN LOSS BY TENURE

The longer a fraudster had worked for a company, the more harm he or she was likely to cause.

- $51,000 < 1 YEAR
- $100,000 1-5 YEARS
- $200,000 6-10 YEARS
- $220,000 > 10 YEARS

Used with permission.

PROVING FRAUD

The vast majority of fraud instances go unpunished. One reason for the lack of convictions is a lack of investigations, with even fewer prosecutions, both of which require the limited resources of law enforcement agencies.

To get a conviction, the prosecution must demonstrate that the lie altered the outcome of a claim for financial gain, and that the misrepresentation was material with intent to deceive. Financial losses aren't always required. Potential loss is sometimes enough. If you tried and failed to rob a bank, after all, you could still be charged with a crime. The same goes for insurance fraud.

Insurance companies are legally required to investigate all suspected fraud. Each state has its own individual statutes, because state governments have a vested interest in weeding out fraud to protect their citizens. To that end, the insurance and self-insurance community maintain a national database in which they store information about all insurance claims, which they can use to cross-check with new claims.

Because insurance companies are on the frontline, they're charged with stamping it out by providing documentation and reporting back to the state. The cost of investigation and litigation to these companies, however, is measured in time and money—a lot of each. Getting a conviction requires finding the lie and proving the lie was material to the case and done with the intent to deceive—each a hurdle to be overcome. So, while they're required to investigate, insurance companies have no control when it comes to litigating suspected fraud cases. This is done at the district attorney level or at each state insurance department's discretion. In most instances, it's easier to simply write off the loss as a cost of doing business, then pass the cost on to the consumer in the form of higher premiums.

In addition to the criminal legal process, there's a separate forum to adjudicate workers' compensation claims, an appeals system with its own judges that holds its own hearings separate from civil and criminal courts. It's important to aggressively fight fraud cases here, because even if the incident doesn't rise to the level of criminal activity, there are malingering and exaggerated cases. Sometimes, injuries aren't as long lasting or severe as the injured worker insists. If properly investigated, the cost of a settlement can get significantly reduced in such cases.

In terms of cost savings, fighting these claims is well worth the effort. Fighting fraud at the appeals court level and in criminal court sends a message that it's not okay to lie. Employers who don't aggressively investigate claims imply that they're soft on fraud, which only exacerbates the problem.

WHY DO INSURANCE RATES INCREASE?

Fraud, even malingering and exaggerated claims, causes insurance rates to rise, but a high frequency of claims in one year can also turn into rising costs that get absorbed by the customer the following year. In other words, insurance rates increase based on the employer's experience modification (XMOD). Insurance companies work under the assumption that past experience is the best predictor of future circumstances.

Doctors and lawyers also figure into the equation. Increased claims frequency means increased medical costs and legal fees. Another major driver is disability benefits, as injured workers require payment for time off work.

A CULTURE OF OPPORTUNITY

A culture of opportunity exists when an employer has lax policies and procedures in documenting and reporting claimed injuries. It can exist in a mom-and-pop business as well as a Fortune 500 company.

The workers' compensation process is guided by specific timetables. The moment a worker says they've been hurt, the clock starts running: the employer and the insurance company have ninety days to investigate that claim without inflicting heavy costs. If a company doesn't take immediate action in response to an injury claim, the entire culture suffers, as other employees realize the company probably doesn't follow other procedures either. Such negligence by an employer also contributes to apathy.

One way employers can reduce opportunity is by establishing a culture in which claims get investigated early. Another method is by establishing rigid safety practices in which employees recognize that a proper protocol exists for all workplace accidents. Awareness is another preventative measure. If you hear about an employee having financial problems at home—the car getting repossessed, the house getting foreclosed—there's now a need, and you can assume there's apathy. All that's left for malfeasance is an opportunity. By being aware of potential abuses, you can stay one step ahead of fraud.

CASE STUDY

The following case provides an example of a culture of opportunity, revealing the real-world actions the employer could have taken to prevent abuse.

A thirty-six-year-old painter named Manny claimed he sustained injuries to his lower back and left hamstring while working on a job. According to his account, he was painting a house when his ladder suddenly folded, and he fell to the wooden floor, landing on his back.

He allegedly sat out the rest of his shift, but he didn't report the incident to his supervisor. He was able to return to work the next day because the pain had subsided, so he didn't think it necessary to tell his supervisor.

Three weeks later, Manny's pain became worse. Rather than report to work, he called in and spoke to his supervisor. He didn't immediately explain the nature of the injury. Instead, he merely said he wasn't feeling well. The supervisor didn't press him on it and recommended he take the day off.

If the supervisor had been more diligent, he would have probed for more information about Manny's condition, trying to determine why he wasn't feeling well and if it was work related. If he had done so, he would have discovered that the injury happened on the job, so he could've sent the proper forms right away, gotten Manny in to see a doctor, and begun interviewing everyone who had been working on the day in question.

The next day, Manny reported to work, but was only able to work an hour or two because of the pain. It would be his last day on the job. The company finally became aware of his "on-the-job injury." They sent him to a doctor, where he received some pain medication, was prescribed light duty, and finally received his insurance claims form. At last, an investigation was started.

During a recorded statement, Manny would later tell the investigator that two coworkers had witnessed the accident. Painters, however, can be transient. The coworkers on that particular job were long gone, and the investigator never got to interview them. That's a problem because the burden is on the employer, not on the injured worker, to prove the person is lying. Furthermore, the more time that passes, the more memories fade and evidence disappears. Even locating the broken ladder proved impossible.

If the culture in the company had been oriented toward fraud prevention, every employee would have known that if someone gets hurt, it must immediately be reported no matter how minor the injury might appear. The fact that no one spoke up about the incident demonstrates the employer wasn't aggressive enough in enforcing injury-reporting best practices. That's why we recommend all incidents, no matter how small or big, be reported.

To wrap up the story, our investigation finally turned up one of the "witnesses." While the man had indeed witnessed the injured worker fall off a ladder, he said it happened two years earlier and for an entirely different employer. According to the witness, Manny had been trying to move the ladder while he was still standing on it. The ladder fell, and so did he. Prior to our interview with this witness, Manny had called him and asked him to tell us the fall had occurred only a few weeks earlier, the date he had given the insurance company.

Manny had a legitimate injury, but it wasn't sustained while working for his current employer. Because the company had a culture of opportunity, Manny felt emboldened to take advantage. Consequently, the company spent a good deal of money investigating the claim.

Such costs can be avoided altogether simply by establishing a better culture from the outset, showing greater awareness of the possibility of fraud, enforcing injury reporting policies, and taking a more aggressive stance in investigating claims.

For a comprehensive list of possible red flags, check out the appendix.

CHAPTER 2

LEGAL REQUIREMENTS

Private investigation companies, insurance companies, and employers are subject to regulations. These include federal, state, and local laws and statutes covering privacy, trespassing, and due process in regard to criminal actions. All of these regulations govern what investigators and insurers can and can't do.

In the state of California, the laws regulating investigators are governed by an agency called the California Bureau of Security and Investigative Services (BSIS), while two statutory systems regulate investigators and insurance adjusters: The Insurance Adjusters Act, and the Private Investigator Act (1994), which came about to control the regulation of licensing, registration, and discipline of private investigators. The portion of the California Business and Professions Code specific to professionally licensed private investigators ranges from 7512 to 7567.

In regard to privacy, private investigators operate differently than ordinary citizens in terms of what they can do during investigations. A private investigator in California must be licensed. Most operate at a higher standard, which means when they violate someone's rights, it may become a civil or criminal matter.

Experienced investigators, HR professionals, and insurance companies understand fully the laws and regulations they have to follow. However, industry professionals need to stay current on new legislation and case law to avoid liability. In this book, I hope to clarify this issue by providing a clear sense of the applicable laws and regulations, particularly in regard to workers' comp investigations.

SPECIAL INVESTIGATIONS UNITS

In order to investigate claims, insurance companies must create a Special Investigations Unit (SIU). In California, the California Code of Regulations, Article 2, Special Investigation Unit Regulations, Section 2698.30, lays out the legal requirement for insurance companies to form a Special Investigations Unit. Of course, requirements vary from state to state, and each state has its own set of nuances on these requirements.

These regulations indicate what must be reported: any suspected fraudulent insurance claim activity. Regardless of the location where the fraud allegedly took place, it must be reported. Specific forms must be filled out within sixty days of the time the insurer believes a fraudulent act was committed. That means companies must act quickly. The idea is to encourage employers, insurance companies, and third-party administrators to create a swift, united front against fraud. If companies don't deal with instances of fraud quickly and aggressively, it might run rampant. That will make premiums rise, which, in turn, will drive up prices for many things throughout the economy.

In the end, out-of-control fraudulent claims can break an insurance company and drive a company to file for bankruptcy. When that happens, open claims get transferred to the state, so taxpayers end up footing the bill. Even with regulations and safety structures in place, the National Insurance Crime Bureau and the Coalition on Insurance Fraud estimate that, nationally, 7 percent of every insurance premium goes toward fighting fraud. It's hard to imagine what that percentage would be without structures in place.

Some states don't fight fraudulent claims as aggressively as others. The State of Arizona, for example, doesn't investigate insurance applicant fraud even on a proportional scale. They don't have to because their relevant laws tend to be pro-employer. It's very tough to beat the system in Arizona. It's not the same in other states. Some have very liberal laws, which make it easier to abuse the system. In New York, for example, an injured employee can pick any doctor they wish. That creates a system that is very employee oriented, and in a state like that, there will need to be more fraud investigations.

States can choose to fight fraudulent claims on the front end by passing pro-employer laws that make it difficult to commit fraud in the first place, or they can fight on the back end during investigations. California has more employee-friendly laws, so they have to fight on the back end by using solid or proven claims management. However, California has for the past fifteen years moved to reduce costs and curb fraud by moving to evidence-based medicine with the passage of Senate Bill 266 and Senate Bill 899 to deal with apportionment and permanent impairment.

FROM DETECTION TO CONVICTION

The first thing the Special Investigations Unit must do is provide training for claims examiners, so they know how to identify suspected fraud. A fraudulent claim might be a post-termination claim where, all of a sudden, the company receives a claim from a person who hasn't worked there in thirty days. Sometimes, it's a small business in which the person filing a claim happens to be the spouse, relative, or friend of the employer.

As soon as a new claim is made, the SIU must collect information from everyone involved. As a matter of precaution, they should run information about the claim through systems such as EAMS, Electronic Adjudication Management System, (https://www.dir.ca.gov/dwc/eams/eams.htm) and claims databases like ISO Claims Search (https://www.verisk.com/insurance/products/claimsearch/), to see what they discover. If anything suspicious turns up, it's time to dig deeper. At that point, the SIU might decide to do a background search on the injured worker, looking at their criminal/civil history and social media—anything that provides a clearer picture. Whether or not they find anything during that deeper search, they should start interviewing people, which usually means outsourcing an investigator. The investigator then interviews the employer, any witnesses, and the injured worker to determine what happened, how it happened, when it happened, and why, as well as specific details around the injury.

If, during this process, the investigator determines that the injury did, in fact, occur on the job or in the course of employment, called AOE/COE (Arising Out of Employment/Course of Employment), then the company should use that information to prevent it from happening again. On the other hand, if any clues, new witnesses, or red flags pop up during that process, it's time to investigate any prior injuries of the injured worker. The investigator might want to find out what medications the individual is taking, which doctors they've seen in the past, and whether or not they go to the gym. If any new witnesses have been identified by this point, they should be interviewed.

At this point, the investigator might want to conduct surveillance. Maybe they want to video the individual to find out what their daily activities look like or what kind of physical activity they are involved in, so they can compare it to the claim. If, during surveillance, the situation looks even more suspicious, then it's time to gather evidence.

If video surveillance turns up evidence to contradict the injury claim, the SIU can send the video to the treating physician, qualified medical examiner (QME), independent medical examiner (IME) or agreed medical examiner (AME). Then, the medical examiner can take a look and see if it's consistent with the nature of the injury and/or restrictions. If there's legitimacy to the claim, the doctor's feedback might at least limit the size of the settlement. However, if the medical examiner determines the video provides evidence that the injured worker is malingering or lying, that can be enough to deny benefits or reduce the demand or settlement. Relevant evidence summarizing the fraud is collected and put into a formal report. In California the form, called the FD-1, Suspected Fraudulent Claim Form, is then submitted to the Department of Insurance or the District Attorney to seek prosecution. Each state has their own forms they require.

A well-run SIU should remain in the loop every step of the way, serving as the quarterback calling the shots on which direction to go with the investigation. Their role is to stamp out fraud claims and abuse by seeking convictions. It should be pointed out, however, that in the state of California, with a population of 30 million, very few fraud convictions actually occur. This is particularly shocking since California has a high number of filed claims. For example, the state recorded just five convictions in June of 2017,[3] and that's a typical month. District attorneys don't enjoy wasting time, so they're only going to take a case if they believe the chances of getting a conviction are high. That, coupled with a small budget, few resources to prosecute, and court backlogs, impact the low rate of fraud convictions.

Consider the following data from the California Department of Insurance *2016 Annual Report to the Commissioner*:[4]

3   California Department of Insurance. "June 2017 Workers' Compensation Fraud Convictions." http://www.insurance.ca.gov/0300-fraud/0100-fraud-division-overview/25-wc-conv/ upload/6-June2017.pdf (accessed May 8, 2018)

4   California Department of Insurance. "2016 Annual Report to the Commissioner." http:// www.insurance.ca.gov/0400-news/0200-studies-reports/0700-commissioner-report/ upload/2016-Annual-Report.pdf (accessed May 14, 2018)

SUSPECTED FRAUDULENT CLAIMS (SFCS) FISCAL YEAR 2015-16
Worker's Compensation—5,380

**THE NUMBER OF CASES REJECTED BY THE FRAUD DIVISION
DUE TO INSUFFICIENT EVIDENCE OR OTHER REASONS -
FISCAL YEAR 2015-16 *(STATUS OF SFCS AS OF 8/22/2016)***
SFCs closed, unassigned due to insufficient evidence—10,434
SFCs closed, unassigned due to insufficient resources—16,154
SFCs closed, unassigned due to other reasons—1,357
SFCs that were assigned to investigators—1,329

**THE NUMBER AND TYPES OF CASES PROSECUTED AS
A RESULT OF FUNDING RECEIVED UNDER INSURANCE
CODE § 1872.86 FISCAL YEAR 2015-16**
SFCs that resulted in conviction or referred to District
Attorney or other Prosecuting Authority—58

AN EFFECTIVE DETERRENT

The benefit of an SIU doesn't come solely from getting a conviction. They also help to stamp out malingering and abuse in other ways. Suppose a claimed injury doesn't show up on an MRI, but the individual still complains about pain and can't do light work. During surveillance, he gets caught lifting his twenty-five-pound child, even though he's not supposed to lift over five pounds.

No judge or jury is ever going to convict someone for lifting their own child, just as they won't convict someone for picking up a gallon of milk or a bag of groceries. From an economic standpoint, the government doesn't want to waste money prosecuting cases when there are gray areas. It's a waste of resources. However, pursuing conviction might discourage others from making similar fraudulent claims.

Prevention is the key. This is true, of course, in any area of law enforcement. People hire security guards to prevent crime from occurring, rather than focusing all of their efforts on trying to convict people after a crime has taken place. By creating an aggressive defense, the SIU sends a signal that they're serious about fraud—that they're going to investigate thoroughly whenever a claim comes up. This creates an effective deterrent.

A well-run defensive strategy works.

CLAIMS FREQUENCY ON THE RISE

Claims frequency has increased in Los Angeles, though the rest of California continues to experience a steady, modest, year-to-year decline. In 2015, estimated indemnity claims per thousand employees per year was 16.1, or 1.6 percent of workers filing claims. California is second in the nation for claims frequency, second only to Delaware.

California doctors follow a course of treatment guidelines from the American College of Occupational and Environmental Medicine (ACOEM).[5] If you have an orthopedic back sprain, the normal course of treatment recommended by the ACOEM could be three weeks off, followed by light duty for another three weeks, then

---

5   American College of Occupation and Environmental Medicine. "Occupational Medicine Practice Guidelines." https://www.acoem.org/practiceguidelines.aspx. (accessed May 10, 2018)

modified duty for three more weeks. That treatment may include six physical therapy treatments and a reasonable amount of pain medication if necessary.

Unfortunately, the cost of healthcare treatment has continued to grow exponentially in this country. If you have a workers' comp claim in California and get an MRI, there is some relief for employers and insurance companies because of state-regulated fee schedules in workers' comp (California Labor Code 5307.1). Healthcare providers must subscribe to a fee schedule and agree to regulated costs. It's important to scrutinize every medical bill, in order to make sure doctors don't overcharge for services. A doctor shouldn't charge $1,100 for an MRI that, according to the Official Medical Fee Schedule (OMFS), should cost under $600.

An aggressive approach to fraud prevention happens in a number of ways: first, through investigations of actual injury claims, and second, by investigating provider fraud, and third, by securitizing treatment plans using utilization review (UR). Utilization review is the process employers or claims administrators use to review and determine if a treatment is medically necessary. All employers or their workers' comp claims administrators are required by law to have a UR program. This program is used to determine whether or not to approve medical treatment recommended by a physician, which must be based on the medical treatment guidelines.[6]

When providers abuse the system, they tend to do so in big numbers because they usually provide fraudulent information for many of their patients. Suddenly, all their patients are having knee problems and need knee replacement surgery. This happens too often, which is why American College of Occupational and Environmental Medicine (ACOEM) guidelines must always be part of an investigation. Going after unscrupulous providers is another way to get a conviction, which helps eliminate abuse.

WHY ARE SO MANY CASES SETTLED?

In general, courts are so inundated with cases that it's now mandatory for judges to require one last conversation between parties in an attempt to come to an agreement before rendering a judgment. Criminal cases, by and large, are plea bargained. Civil cases often require mandatory settlement conferences and arbitration. The same is true of workers' compensation cases. Judges want parties to solve their problems before a ruling becomes necessary.

Often, the defense attorney will present the judge with

---

6   State of California Department of Insurance. "Utilization review." https://www.dir.ca.gov/dwc/UR_Main.htm. (accessed on May 10, 2018)

video surveillance, or some other evidence contrary to the claim. The injured worker's applicant attorney will counter that the evidence does not accurately represent the situation. Then the judge will encourage the two parties to work something out, at which point both parties will attempt to reach a settlement that both are comfortable with.

Most cases play out this way. Courts simply can't hear every case all the way to hearing because, along with the appeals that might follow, it clogs up the court system.

LEGAL REQUIREMENTS TOWARD THE INJURED WORKER

When someone gets injured on the job, the employer and insurance company are required to provide medical treatment. It's in the best interest of the employer to get the injured employee back to work, but this is not required. If the injured employee can't get back to work, the employer and insurance company are required to compensate for the amount of disability. For example, if someone is 15 percent disabled, the insurance company is obligated to compensate them for the 15 percent disability rating. Permanent impairment isn't paid for lost wages, but for each percent of permanent impairment sustained by the injured employee. For this reason, an investigator will attempt to get a better picture of the injured worker's claim before negotiating a settlement, so they can come to court or arbitration armed with a defense.

There are specific case laws and statutory laws that regulate investigations. If an investigation company is hired by an SIU department or insurance company, any inappropriate actions or unlawful activity on the investigator's part can be used against them, and they can be held civilly liable. That's why we're so careful to conduct every investigation ethically.

A company shouldn't investigate a claim simply because a claim is expensive. There must be suspicion of fraud. Fair claims settlement practices regulations (California Code of Regulations, Title 10, Chapter 5, Subchapter 7.5) ensure fair claims settlements for injured workers while providing a means for effectively, efficiently, and equitably settling claims. It requires everyone to play fair.

SIXTEEN SETTLEMENT PRACTICES

Section 790.03(h) of the California Insurance Code lists sixteen settlement practices that are considered to be unfair practices when knowingly committed on a single occasion or performed with enough frequency to indicate a general business practice.[7]

---

7   California State Legislature. "ARTICLE 6.5. Unfair Practices [790 - 790.15]." California Legislative Information. http://leginfo.legislature.ca.gov/faces/codes_displayText. xhtml?lawCode=INS&division=1.&title=&part=2.&chapter=1.&article=6.5. (accessed on May 8, 2018)

(a) Making, issuing, circulating, or causing to be made, issued or circulated, any estimate, illustration, circular, or statement misrepresenting the terms of any policy issued or to be issued or the benefits or advantages promised thereby or the dividends or share of the surplus to be received thereon, or making any false or misleading statement as to the dividends or share of surplus previously paid on similar policies, or making any misleading representation or any misrepresentation as to the financial condition of any insurer, or as to the legal reserve system upon which any life insurer operates, or using any name or title of any policy or class of policies misrepresenting the true nature thereof, or making any misrepresentation to any policyholder insured in any company for the purpose of inducing or tending to induce the policyholder to lapse, forfeit, or surrender his or her insurance.

(b) Making or disseminating or causing to be made or disseminated before the public in this state, in any newspaper or other publication, or any advertising device, or by public outcry or proclamation, or in any other manner or means whatsoever, any statement containing any assertion, representation, or statement with respect to the business of insurance or with respect to any person in the conduct of his or her insurance business, which is untrue, deceptive, or misleading, and which is known, or which by the exercise of reasonable care should be known, to be untrue, deceptive, or misleading.

(c) Entering into any agreement to commit, or by any concerted action committing, any act of boycott, coercion, or intimidation resulting in or tending to result in unreasonable restraint of, or monopoly in, the business of insurance.

(d) Filing with any supervisory or other public official, or making, publishing, disseminating, circulating, or delivering to any person, or placing before the public, or causing directly or indirectly, to be made, published, disseminated, circulated, delivered to any person, or placed before the public any false statement of financial condition of an insurer with intent to deceive.

(e) Making any false entry in any book, report, or statement of any insurer with intent to deceive any agent or examiner lawfully appointed to examine into its condition or into any of its affairs, or any public official to whom the insurer is required by law to report, or who has authority by law to examine into its condition or into any of its affairs, or, with like intent, willfully omitting to make a true entry of any material fact pertaining to the business of the insurer in any book, report, or statement of the insurer.

(f)(1) Making or permitting any unfair discrimination between individuals of the same class and equal expectation of life in the rates charged for any contract of life insurance or of life annuity or in the dividends or other benefits payable thereon, or in any other of the terms and conditions of the contract.

(f)(2) This subdivision shall be interpreted, for any contract of ordinary life insurance or individual life annuity applied for and issued on or after January 1, 1981, to require differentials based upon the sex of the individual insured or annuitant in the rates or dividends or benefits, or any combination thereof. This requirement is satisfied if those differentials are substantially supported by valid pertinent data segregated by sex, including, but not limited to, mortality data segregated by sex.

(f)(3) However, for any contract of ordinary life insurance or individual life annuity applied for and issued on or after January 1, 1981, but before the compliance date, in lieu of those differentials based on data segregated by sex, rates, or dividends or benefits, or any combination thereof, for ordinary life insurance or individual life annuity on a female life may be calculated as follows: (A) according to an age not less than three years nor more than six years younger than the actual age of the female insured or female annuitant, in the case of a contract of ordinary life insurance with a face value greater than five thousand dollars ($5,000) or a contract of individual life annuity; and (B) according to an age not more than six years younger than the actual age of the female insured, in the case of a contract of ordinary life insurance with a face value of five thousand dollars ($5,000) or less. "Compliance date" as used in this paragraph shall mean the date or dates established as the operative date or dates by future amendments to this code directing and authorizing life insurers to use a mortality table containing mortality data segregated by sex for the calculation of adjusted premiums and present values for nonforfeiture benefits and valuation reserves as specified in Sections 10163.1 and 10489.2 or successor sections.

(f)(4) Notwithstanding the provisions of this subdivision, sex-based differentials in rates or dividends or benefits, or any combination thereof, shall not be required for (A) any contract of life insurance or life annuity issued pursuant to arrangements which may be considered terms, conditions, or privileges of employment as these terms are used in Title VII of the Civil Rights Act of 1964 (Public Law 88-352), as amended, and (B) tax-sheltered annuities for employees of public schools or of tax-exempt organizations described in Section 501(c)(3) of the Internal Revenue Code 1.

(g) Making or disseminating, or causing to be made or disseminated, before the public in this state, in any newspaper or other publication, or any other advertising device, or by public outcry or proclamation, or in any other manner or means whatever, whether directly or by implication, any statement that a named insurer, or named insurers, are members of the California Insurance Guarantee Association, or insured against insolvency as defined in Section

119.5. This subdivision shall not be interpreted to prohibit any activity of the California Insurance Guarantee Association or the commissioner authorized, directly or by implication, by Article 14.2 (commencing with Section 1063).

(h) Knowingly committing or performing with such frequency as to indicate a general business practice any of the following unfair claims settlement practices:

(1) Misrepresenting the claimant's pertinent facts or insurance policy provisions relating to any coverages at issue.

(2) Failing to acknowledge and act reasonably promptly upon communications with respect to claims arising under insurance policies.

(3) Failing to adopt and implement reasonable standards for the prompt investigation and processing of claims arising under insurance policies.

(4) Failing to affirm or deny coverage of claims within a reasonable time after proof of loss requirements have been completed and submitted by the insured.

(5) Not attempting in good faith to effectuate prompt, fair, and equitable settlements of claims in which liability has become reasonably clear.

(6) Compelling insureds to institute litigation to recover amounts due under an insurance policy by offering substantially less than the amounts ultimately recovered in actions brought by the insureds, when the insureds have made claims for amounts reasonably similar to the amounts ultimately recovered.

(7) Attempting to settle a claim by an insured for less than the amount to which a reasonable person would have believed he or she was entitled by reference to written or printed advertising material accompanying or made part of an application.

(8) Attempting to settle claims on the basis of an application that was altered without notice to, or knowledge or consent of, the insured, his or her representative, agent, or broker.

(9) Failing, after payment of a claim, to inform insureds or beneficiaries, upon request by them, of the coverage under which payment has been made.

(10) Making known to insureds or claimants a practice of the insurer of appealing from arbitration awards in favor of insureds or claimants for the purpose of compelling them to accept settlements or compromises less than the amount awarded in arbitration.

(11) Delaying the investigation or payment of claims by

requiring an insured, claimant, or the physician of either, to submit a preliminary claim report, and then requiring the subsequent submission of formal proof of loss forms, both of which submissions contain substantially the same information.

(12) Failing to settle claims promptly, where liability has become apparent, under one portion of the insurance policy coverage in order to influence settlements under other portions of the insurance policy coverage.

(13) Failing to provide promptly a reasonable explanation of the basis relied on in the insurance policy, in relation to the facts or applicable law, for the denial of a claim or for the offer of a compromise settlement.

(14) Directly advising a claimant not to obtain the services of an attorney.

(15) Misleading a claimant as to the applicable statute of limitations.

(16) Delaying the payment or provision of hospital, medical, or surgical benefits for services provided with respect to acquired immune deficiency syndrome or AIDS-related complex for more than sixty days after the insurer has received a claim for those benefits, where the delay in claim payment is for the purpose of investigating whether the

condition preexisted the coverage. However, this sixty-day period shall not include anytime during which the insurer is awaiting a response for relevant medical information from a healthcare provider.

(i) Canceling or refusing to renew a policy in violation of Section 676.10.

(j) Holding oneself out as representing, constituting, or otherwise providing services on behalf of the California Health Benefit Exchange established pursuant to Section 100500 of the Government Code without a valid agreement with the California Health Benefit Exchange to engage in those activities.

ETHICAL STANDARDS

The case *Brady v. Maryland 1963* established the ethical standards that investigators need to follow in accumulating evidence. As part of that process, any video evidence must be turned over to the injured worker and his or her lawyer. Other cases, such as *Pittenger v. Collection Agency* and *Chodur v. Edmonds*, have specifically prohibited all forms of fraud, deception, betrayal, absence of integrity, and disposition to cheat or deceive on the part of the investigator. The Private Investigators Act mandates that the bureau has the right to revoke someone's license who's been convicted of a felony or a crime involving unethical behavior.

Special Investigation Units are a legal requirement for insurance companies. According to the California Department of Insurance:[8]

> The primary responsibility of the California Department of Insurance (CDI) Special Investigative Unit (SIU) Compliance Review Program is to audit insurers and to evaluate regulatory and statutory compliance regarding the establishment, maintenance, and operation of the insurer's SIU program. The Compliance Review Program also distributes, monitors, and evaluates the SIU Annual Reports filed by approximately 1,100 insurers each year.
>
> California licensed insurers are required by California Insurance Code Sections 1875.20-24 and California Code of Regulations, Title 10, Sections 2698.30 -.43 to establish and maintain Special Investigative Units that identify and refer suspected insurance fraud to CDI (and the California County District Attorney's Office for workers' compensation only).

Many TPAs also choose to either voluntarily create SIU departments or outsource to an investigation company. The purpose is to stay in compliance with state law but also to reduce fraud. SIU departments directly interface with claims departments to help identify, report, and fight

---

8   California Department of Insurance. "SIU Compliance Review Program." http://www.insurance.ca.gov/0300-fraud/0100-fraud-division-overview/12-siu/ (accessed May 14, 2018)

fraud. Together, SIU departments and claims professionals refer suspected fraud cases to investigators.

SIUs don't typically conduct recorded statements or surveillance. That's where private investigation firms like ours come in. We become the enforcement and investigative arm of an SIU, doing all of the field work, while they monitor and fund the work. If we produce evidence that shows their initial suspicion was accurate, the SIU collects our evidence, reports it to the State Department of Insurance, and uses it in defense of the claim.

Employers must understand that when they use an insurance company or TPA's SIU, they're often hiring outside investigators to do the actual footwork, and the investigators they hire had better understand the applicable laws that protect the privacy of injured workers filing claims. For example, no one (insurance company, TPA, DA, etc.) should ever ask an investigator to trespass on the injured worker's property.

"Please, go to this sixty-acre gated ranch and drive onto the property to get video surveillance of them."

That kind of request is not acceptable, and the investigator must understand what privacy and trespassing look like, to avoid creating problems for the employer, insurance company, TPA, DA, or anyone else.

CHAPTER 3

THE CLAIMS DEPARTMENT

A client hospital in Southern California had a nurse who had been working in the hospital for five or six years when she claimed she began developing an allergic reaction to latex. At that time, hospitals didn't recognize the side effects of latex, and they hadn't started offering non-latex gloves, like they do today.

Latex comes from a specific type of tree found in the rainforest, which is manufactured into a rubbery, pliable material. Some healthcare workers who had to wear it all day, every day, started developing allergic reactions.

In this case, the nurse claimed that after five or six years, she could no longer work at the hospital because she had developed a latex allergy at age thirty-five. Since this happened during the early days of latex allergy claims, it caused a lot of confusion. Third-party administrators and insurance companies raised many questions.

Since she already worked in a hospital, they decided to send her to their doctor. Doctors typically treat allergies by running tests to see what the patient is allergic to. At the time, they generally tested for sixty different allergens, but latex wasn't one of them. Since the employer hadn't seen any prior latex allergy claims, it was the perfect opportunity to open a claims investigation to learn more. This allowed them to interview the nurse, find out about any prior allergies, and ask when she first noticed she was having problems at work with her hands.

As expected, she claimed the allergies developed on her hands over time. She said that she started having outbreaks an hour or so after she put on latex gloves. Sometimes, it happened when she went home at night. As a result of these regular outbreaks, she couldn't perform her normal job duties.

The hospital offered to accommodate her. "If you return to work, we'll move you to a position that doesn't require wearing gloves, and when you come into contact with patients, we'll make sure you have non-latex gloves."

They provided her with non-latex gloves, but she claimed that her allergies had gotten so bad that she couldn't even be at the hospital without having an outbreak. Now, they faced having to pay her to take off work completely, and if she were genuinely precluded from working, there could be could be at least two years of temporary disability (TD) payments for the hospital, according to California law (other states vary). The situation was similar to a firefighter who has inhaled smoke for thirty years on the job and then develops lung cancer, or a warehouse worker who does a lot of heavy lifting for years and then develops a back problem.

The hospital did their best to accommodate the nurse, but returning to work wasn't an option for her. They paid the nurse TD benefits, so she could recover from her injury. No matter how they tried to accommodate her, she would not agree to come back to work. Finally, a claims manager said, "Why don't we hire Apex to conduct covert surveillance, so we can see what life looks life for our injured worker?" At that point, the claims investigation became a surveillance investigation.

When an injured worker won't accept accommodations to return to work, that is often a signal to the employer and insurance company that the person has some other motivation. A number of red flags emerged during the claims investigation. The injured worker was also difficult to reach; calls always went to voicemail, and she'd call back only hours later. We found it increasingly hard to contact her, and she was unwilling to accept modified duty.

CONDUCTING SURVEILLANCE

We conducted surveillance and collected samples of anything she came in contact with. If she went out to a fast food restaurant, we took samples of the lid, the straw, and the cup she drank out of and sent them off to a lab. We photographed her shoes, bought a pair of the same brand, and sent those to a lab. When we did that, we learned that the insides of the shoes are glued down with latex, and the rubber around the shoe was also latex. We talked to her car manufacturer and learned there was latex in multiple places throughout the car, including the seats, carpet, headliner, and the leather-wrapped steering wheel.

At that point in the claim, she began insisting that things had gotten so bad, she was living like the boy in the bubble. She said she had a difficult time going anywhere where there was latex. Some of the claimed symptoms included rash, severe headaches, swelling, and difficulty breathing to the point that it was almost asthmatic. She said her airways felt like they were getting more constricted, and she paid for latex removal throughout her home. She also had to buy special air filters to eliminate the reaction.

However, during our investigation, we saw no evidence of any of that. On the contrary, she seemed to be living a normal life. When we asked her about this, she couldn't fully explain it, although she was careful not to blatantly lie. At best, she misled, but we found no evidence of a latex allergy and no evidence that her life was disrupted to such a degree that she couldn't do any work. In fact, we could show evidence to the contrary.

Unfortunately, we didn't have enough to get a fraud conviction, but we did determine that she could perform her daily tasks with a non-latex glove in an environment with airborne latex. There was no reason she couldn't go back to work with some reasonable accommodations.

SETTLING THE CLAIM

She opted not to go back to work, but the hospital ultimately settled the claim for far less than she wanted. They chose to settle because we didn't have enough direct evidence of fraud. Fortunately, they didn't blindly accept the claim and pay out ten times the amount.

In the end, the case came down to a single question, "What was the cumulative effect of her six-year exposure to latex, if any?"

Her argument was that it was so debilitating she was precluded from working or living a normal life. She claimed to have become 100 percent disabled and unable to work again for the rest of her life. Settling a case at 100 percent disability would have meant paying a large settlement, putting filters in her house, providing a non-latex mattress, paying for hospital visits and treatments, and providing any other accommodations she needed for the rest of her life. However, since the client started an investigation early, and we used some creativity to find out what she was eating and wearing, where she was living, and what kind of car she was driving, we discovered that she had far more tolerance for latex than she claimed.

It's possible she truly did have a latex allergy. There was no direct evidence to prove she lied, but she had clearly exaggerated. That's a common problem. Workers' comp claims often get exaggerated.

EXAGGERATING THE CLAIM

For example, someone's car might get broken into, and the thief shatters the windshield. The vehicle owner sees the damage and thinks, "My insurance policy has a $500 deductible. I might as well claim that my expensive leather jacket also got stolen out of the car, so I can get enough from insurance to cover the deductible."

Of course, latex allergies are looked at very differently now, because doctors have a greater understanding of what the typical symptoms are: hives, itching, runny nose, asthma.

Fibromyalgia used to be the catchall for people filing claims. If the person was savvy, you couldn't catch them in a lie and they would usually get a settlement. Fibromyalgia affects the muscles and soft tissue, with symptoms that include chronic muscle pain, muscle fatigue, sleep problems, tender spots, and trigger points. Since it affects soft tissues, it doesn't show up on an X-ray, MRI, or blood test.

About ten years ago, California passed workers' comp reform to change the way the law regards treatment and diagnosis, adopting guidelines from the American Medical Association (AMA) and the American College of Occupational and Environmental Medicine (ACOEM), which has created the gold standard for guidelines in effective treatment of occupational injuries and illness, as well as establishing permanent impairment ratings. The ACOEM's unique, evidence-based guidelines focus on getting employees back to work using medical diagnosis and treatment.

Once the industry shifted to evidence-based treatment plans, it threw out a lot of the soft-tissue, imaginary, phantom injury claims. Anyone who had settled their case before was thankful they beat the wire. Because of the ACOEM guidelines, the number of subjective claims and fibromyalgia claims has greatly diminished.

Sophisticated doctors can tell when a patient is faking their symptoms—giving fake grimaces or a half-strength grip. A doctor might even be armed with surveillance video contradicting the injured person's claim. The insurance company, third-party administrator, employer, or even the person's treating physician will want to get that footage into the hands of whomever is performing the evaluation. After all, if a doctor sees video contrary to the patient's claim, they're going to send that person back to work.

DAY ONE—THE INJURY HAPPENS

This is how a claim is supposed to work, assuming the employer understands the injured worker's rights and the injured worker understands the employer's procedures when an injury occurs.

It all begins, of course, when a worker gets injured. If they are conscious, they have an obligation to report the injury to their superior immediately. The injured worker should then receive treatment. The employer must gather as much information as possible about how the injury happened, why it happened, and who saw it. For a minor injury, first aid should be applied first, and then the person can be sent to urgent care, if needed or if medical care is requested by the injured employee. For more serious injuries, the employer should call 911 (if the injury is life-threatening), or the worker should be taken to a hospital right away.

If the injured worker is able, he or she must fill out specific forms, as must the employer. These specific forms vary from state to state. The workers' compensation form generally includes a description of how the injury occurred. Though not required, this should be a general practice for all employers who want to combat insurance fraud.

Once filled out, both the employer's and the injured worker's forms should go to the insurance company or claims administrator. However, if they only receive the employer's form, that's enough to start the claims process. Injured workers have many rights, one of which is that their claim must be handled in a timely manner. They must be provided with medical treatment as soon as possible, and the employer must pay for the treatment and provide accommodations, if accommodations are available. All of these things must occur within a certain amount of time. Individual states usually have a specific number of days or weeks in which these steps must be taken. If employers provide adequate care, compensation, and accommodations, as well as a fair claims process, many problems can be avoided down the road. The goal is to make it a fair system for everyone.

When a claim isn't handled in a time-sensitive manner, it

becomes harder for the insurance company or employer to investigate because there's a time frame in which an investigation should take place. In California, the employer must accept, reject, or delay a decision regarding an injury claim within fourteen days of receiving the claim form. If the claim is put on delay, the employer has ninety days to accept or reject the claim. If they fail to do so by then, the injury is presumed compensable and the employer is barred from presenting any evidence to the contrary that could have been obtained during the ninety-day period. In addition, during this delay period, the employer is required to provide up to $10,000 worth of medical care. They are not, however, required to pay temporary disability benefits for wage loss during this delay period.

In one instance, an employee had just been given a final warning about their poor performance. She was told explicitly that if she didn't change, she would be fired. The next day, the worker went to her supervisor, crying, and claimed she had hurt her back trying to lift something. It happened at a retail store, but no one witnessed it. The worker was genuinely crying, but it was possible that she was distressed over potentially losing her job.

These kinds of stories are not uncommon. Some employers are afraid to fire a worker once they've made a workers' comp claim because they don't want to get sued for acting in retaliation. Often, they will put the termination on hold until they work through the claim.

If everyone simply follows the rules immediately following an injury, many claims will be prevented. It's not enough to tell someone about an injury. The worker must follow procedures and fill out the correct forms. The employer must also fill out the correct forms. Human Resources should be informed of any work-related incident, and they should provide the correct forms to the injured employee. Every employer will vary depending on who is responsible for handling work-related injuries. If workers are out on a job site, they should send an email, if they have access, or place a call immediately, and they must be directed to the appropriate healthcare facility. The necessity of following all proper procedures must be continually reemphasized.

Remember, the employer has ninety days to make a determination about whether to accept or deny, so once the injury occurs, the clock starts ticking. If an employer fails to follow their own procedures and the procedures the insurance company requires, they are wasting valuable time.

Stop everything and start talking to people. Speak to as many witnesses as possible. Collect the video before it gets erased. If there were coworkers on the same shift that day, immediately ask everyone on duty, "Did you see anything?" Even if they say no, at least it's documented that no one saw the incident. If they did, get their account of the incident as soon as possible. There's another form that witnesses can fill out. Memories fade fast, and stories sometimes differ, so make sure every witness writes down their version of events. This will become important if there's a deposition months or years later.

DAY TWO—A CLAIMS INVESTIGATION BEGINS

On day two, the claims examiner starts gathering all relevant information to determine whether or not the claim is going to be accepted or denied. They listen to the employer's account of the event, as well as any witnesses, and they also listen to the injured employee's account of the event, if the employee hasn't yet obtained legal counsel. They might also begin looking at the claims history of the injured person to see if they have any open claims from current or past employers.

Essentially, the claims examiner is already investigating the claim at this point. However, once they reach a point where they need someone to provide expert advice on a particular subject, to physically go out and talk to people, perform surveillance, or pull records, that's when they consider outsourcing to a private investigation company.

Generally, claims examiners and risk managers work

at this point to corroborate or refute any red flags. With the worker mentioned earlier who had received a final warning about her poor performance, the fact that she was already facing disciplinary action creates a red flag, particularly since the supervisor threatened to fire her if she didn't improve. When a worker facing imminent disciplinary action and termination files a subjective, no-witness, back injury claim the next day, that is always a red flag, and the claim should be delayed immediately.

On day two, it's time to start asking more detailed questions. Now that the claim is open, all information must be gathered from the Workers' Compensation Claim Form (DWC-1) and the Employer's Report of Occupational Injury or Illness (Form 5020). Note: Every employer is required to file a complete report of every occupational injury or illness to each employee that results in lost time beyond the date of injury or illness or which requires medical treatment beyond first aid.

It's no different than if you get into a car accident today and file a claim with your insurance company, they will have the adjuster call you the same or very next day. They will want to see the police report, any pictures of the damage, and then they will schedule a meeting so someone can look at the car itself. If another party was involved in the accident, they will want to know if that individual had insurance. What the insurance company won't tell you is that they're already searching your DMV record and claims history because the investigation has already begun.

THE CLAIM GOES ON AND ON

At this point, the danger is that the claim goes on and on. The severity, cost, and potential length of a claim will influence how aggressively the claim should be pursued. For example, in the case of the latex allergy, the injured worker was facing a lifetime disability. At the time, permanent impairment ratings were calculated based on a number of factors, including how old the person was at the time of injury, their life expectancy, current wages, earning capacity, occupation, education, future employment, and permanent restrictions. The injured worker was a thirty-five-year-old female living in California, which gave her a life expectancy of 84.

Today in California, AMA guidelines are used in determining permanent impairment ratings. According the American Medical Association, they created these guidelines by using "a consensus-derived percentage estimate of loss of activity, which reflects severity of impairment for a given health condition, and the degree of associated limitations in terms of activities of daily living (ADLs)."[9]

---

9 Rondinelli, Robert, MD, PhD. "AMA Guides to the Evaluation of Permanent Impairment – 6th Edition" https://www.lexisnexis.com/documents/pdf/20090727114916_large.pdf. (accessed May 10, 2018)

In another case, a worker lost a thumb in an accident involving a conveyer belt. The permanent impairment guidelines in AMA Guides to the Evaluation of Permanent Impairment Permanent Impairment – 6th Edition indicate what specific body parts are worth depending on the specific nature of the work. In this case, the amount might be set at $11,700. If the worker needed a thumb in order to do their job, then the amount would be higher.

A nurse who develops a latex injury will have a high claim because their job requires them to be around latex all the time. In this specific case, the nurse worked in prenatal intensive care, so constant exposure to latex was a given. This drove up the claim even further.

Insurance companies take every claim seriously, but, as you can imagine, a case in which hundreds of thousands or even millions of dollars are at stake will be a high priority. In the case of the missing thumb, five witnesses saw the accident occur, so it's a strong claim. It was easy for the insurance company to decide to settle, providing disability payments, treatment, and physical therapy for the worker.

When a case is ambiguous, where the company faces huge losses, they will want to dig deeper. It may not be worth digging deeper into the case of the worker who lost his thumb, considering the witnesses' accounts of the incident. The investigator could test to see if there was alcohol or drugs in his system, but if there wasn't, that will probably be the end of the investigation. On the other hand, let's suppose a truck driver mows down thirty cars on the highway at three in the morning. In that case, the investigation will almost certainly look beyond whether or not the driver had alcohol or drugs in his system. Investigators would speak to countless witnesses, conduct an accident reconstruction, collect highway patrol reports, and look for third-party liability.

As part of the disability rating, the cost of the latex allergy claim is also going to increase because of something called "loss of earning capacity," which is used in about a dozen states. This involves predicting the injured worker's ability to earn money in the future. The most important factor in assessing this is the extent of the injury, but the worker's individual circumstances will also come into play.

THE CASE ENDS UP IN LITIGATION

In California, workers' comp cases are adjudicated by the Workers' Compensation Appeals Board (WCAB), which assists in resolving disputes that arise in connection with claims for workers' compensation benefits. The goal of WCAB is to minimize the adverse impact of work-related injuries on employees and employers.

In most insurance companies, a risk manager works hard

to reduce risk through education, safety training, and good claims management. First aid training can help prevent injuries from becoming long-term disabilities. After all, if a worker cuts his finger and doesn't receive immediate treatment, it could become infected, which might affect the whole arm, leading to a more serious claim.

Along with education and safety training, aggressive claims investigations help to prevent potential problems from slipping through the cracks. Employers, supervisors, and managers must understand the seriousness of all such claims and carefully follow procedures that enable insurance companies to stay on top of them.

Even when an injured worker has a legitimate claim, if they sense the employer doesn't care about them or that no effort is being made to provide the best possible treatment, they can feel wronged. That increases the likelihood that a worker will litigate, and the minute a claim gets litigated, the cost of the claim goes up. Data makes this clear, but it doesn't take a rocket scientist to understand that once lawyers get involved, prices start to climb exponentially. After all, lawyer fees aren't going to come out of the injured worker's pocket; the law requires that additional money come from the insurer. In a way, the cost of legal fees does come out of the injured worker's pocket, since their attorney receives 9 to 15 percent of the total award the injured employee receives. Note: attorneys' fees in California workers' compensation cases must be approved by the Workers' Compensation Appeals Board.

Preventing a first-aid case from turning into an indemnity claim reduces waste and abuses of the system. The value and return on investment are well worth it. Bear in mind, judges would prefer that all parties resolve their own problems, which is why they often require mandatory settlement conferences for arbitration. This alleviates pressure on the courts and allows courts to hear more cases.

Even if a case doesn't go to trial, evidence from the investigation will play a major role during negotiation and could have a huge impact on the settlement. Video evidence, for example, might demonstrate that a claim for permanent impairment is too high. On the other hand, if an injured worker claiming permanent impairment is seen on camera shopping at the mall, dancing, or playing golf, their lawyer might be able to convince a judge that such activity was necessary and not a reflection of the true severity of their injury. These kinds of situations aren't often definitive. A judge might rule in favor of the injured worker, even in the face of contradictory evidence, so letting the judge rule on a claim may be a bigger risk than dealing with it through negotiation.

AN OUNCE OF PREVENTION

As the old saying goes, an ounce of prevention is worth a pound of cure. If company culture is lax about workers' comp, if supervisors and managers aren't meticulous when it comes to filing claims, then the company should expect higher claims.

When workers recognize that their employer takes all workers' comp claims seriously, they will be less likely to abuse the system. A worker should have a clear understanding of how safe practices are good for their paycheck, how they protect the long-term prospects of the company, and spare coworkers from sharing the burden. They should be fully trained on how to report an injury, where to get treatment, and what their rights and benefits are. When an injury happens, they should be able to trust that management is going to take care of them, get them the right doctors, and help them get back to work, even if accommodations need to be made.

When all of that happens, workers feel like they can trust their employer to look out for their best interests, and that creates a culture of accountability. This, in turn, goes a long way toward reducing the number of fraudulent and exaggerated claims. When legitimate claims happen, workers are also less likely to seek legal representation, which reduces costs.

A large retail company, which we shall not name, is currently going through many changes. They have a relatively new CEO and CMO, so many workers are nervous about the restructuring that is taking place. Big changes make workers nervous, so it is imperative that risk management stays on top of all potential problems because when workers get nervous, they may start looking for a backup plan. Company culture plays an extremely important role in risk management during these kinds of transitions.

When it comes to insurance, employers can handle the expense in a couple of ways. They might choose a plan with a high deductible, paying for claims under $300,000 out of pocket. In that case, the majority of claims come right out of the bottom line, with only the larger claims being picked up by the insurance company.

A smaller company might not be able to afford a large deductible, so they will pay a higher premium. The danger is that the frequency of claims will drive up the cost of the premium. This is another reason why it's so important for employers and insurance companies to work together. After all, a worker might have some loyalty to the company, but they won't have loyalty to the insurance company. They might not want to hurt their company, but most people have no qualms about hurting an insurance company, despite the fact that higher premiums can directly slash company benefits or wages.

To prevent this, insurance companies and employers must work together to manage claims. If the employer does everything right, but the insurance company drops the ball, the employer may suffer. Let's suppose the insurance company calculates the cost and decides to settle the claim as fast as possible, without hiring lawyers or investigators. What can the employer do? They might want to fight or investigate the claim to prevent their premium from going up, but insurance companies sometimes have all the power.

Let's suppose we're talking about a small plumbing company with only ten employees. They care about their workers and always try to treat them right. They understand the policy when it comes to filing a claim, so when an injury occurs, they fill out all necessary paperwork and send it to the insurance company. The insurance company decides to take an aggressive approach in getting treatment for the injured worker, making the process difficult for the worker. To complicate matters, the employer expresses concern over what seem like red flags, yet the insurance company seems disinterested in pursuing an investigation.

This kind of situation isn't unusual. Employers frequently complain about insurance companies refusing to investigate, even in the face of red flags. When deductibles are high, employers must push the envelope in getting investigations started.

THE MAJOR PLAYERS IN AN INSURANCE CLAIM

The insurance company or a third-party administrator (TPA) bears responsibility for administering and processing a claim. They are also communicating between the employer, injured worker, witnesses, and doctors. They might have to hire an attorney to represent the employer and insurance company, but they may also deal with the attorney representing the injured worker.

If there's a language barrier, the insurance company will have to hire a translator to communicate with the injured worker. This is often true even in cases where the worker speaks English as a second language. A Filipino worker might feel more comfortable communicating in Tagalog, and if that's the case, the insurance company is required to pay for the translation work. If the worker is unable to drive to get to doctor appointments or physical therapy, they might have to arrange transportation.

It's important to look into the worker's background at the outset. To do this, the insurance company hires a private investigator. As the claim proceeds, the insurance company will also need to hire a permanent impairment rating company to determine the value of the settlement. If the injured worker needs an MRI, they'll have to pay for that, too.

At the same time, they have to make sure they hit all of the benchmarks in their own claims administration process, not missing any dates. Missing dates during the workers' comp process can result in financial penalties from the appeals board. If the insurance company fails to pay any doctor bills, that could also result in penalties.

According to the California Code of Regulations, "When payment of compensation has been unreasonably delayed or refused, either prior to or subsequent to the issuance of an award, the amount of the payment unreasonably delayed or refused shall be increased up to 25 percent or up to ten thousand dollars ($10,000), whichever is less. In any proceeding under this section, the appeals board shall use its discretion to accomplish a fair balance and substantial justice between the parties."[10]

Investigators are hired to do a variety of things. As we mentioned earlier, some insurance companies and third-party administrators have an internal Special Investigations Unit. At a minimum, every organization has someone who is responsible for managing, outsourcing, or internally investigating claims. Generally, most insurance companies don't have significant in-house investigations. They usually hire outside investigators to handle any serious

---

10 State of California Department of Industrial Relations. "Division 1. Department of Industrial Relations. Chapter 4.5 Division of Workers' Compensation." https://www.dir.ca.gov/t8/10112_2.html (accessed May 10, 2018)

investigation, handling only cursory investigations, such as claims history, internally.

An investigator will look up the injured worker's claims history and criminal history. They might look for any social media profiles to see what information can be gleaned from the worker's posts. They will speak to witnesses face-to-face, and they might even visit the home of the person filing a claim. If the injured worker has a military background, they might check military records, looking at discharge papers and any claims made while serving in the military. They will conduct surveillance to document the injured worker's level of physical activity.

Even with an outside investigator, employers continue to play an important role, providing a resume of the injured worker, photographs, gathering witnesses, offering any clues or rumors that might shed light on the situation. If a piece of equipment was involved in the injury, maintenance records will be helpful, as they will reveal who was responsible for that piece of equipment. A conveyer belt, for example, might be maintained by the conveyer belt company. Maybe that company missed something during maintenance and is responsible for the injury.

Even in a legitimate claim, all of this is vital because it will influence the settlement and could reduce costs. Ultimately, the workers' comp system is designed to take care of injured workers. The system was put in place at a time when companies didn't offer healthcare and the government lacked a safety net. It's important to make sure all legitimate claims are paid for and that workers are treated and returned to work as soon as possible.

WHAT INSURANCE PROFESSIONALS NEED TO KNOW

Insurance professionals need to understand the adjudication process. It's a complicated path in which many things have to happen. What does the adjudication process look like, and what role does investigation play from start to finish?

At the outset of a claim, a background check and a social media investigation might be called for. If any red flags turn up, if there's a language barrier, or if the claims examiner can't get in touch with the person filing a claim, they may consider bringing in an outside investigator. However, they need to have a clear understanding of when to use an outside investigator and what the goal is.

Maybe the investigator needs to literally go and knock on the front door of the worker's house to ask the worker questions. Maybe they need to canvas medical facilities or pharmacies in order to acquire more information about their medical history, looking for evidence of prior injuries and treatment. Pharmacies don't provide the investigator with specific information about which prescriptions they provided, but they might be willing to provide confirmation that they have filled prescriptions for someone, which is HIPAA compliant. If the injured worker had a gym membership, the investigator might want to recommend that the defense attorney subpoena gym membership records or, at least, question the individual about it during a deposition, along with specific questions about prescriptions.

It's difficult to predict which direction an investigation will go from that point, but it's important for an insurance professional to understand how investigations fit into every stage of the process. Once the injured worker reaches the end of treatment, they might claim they have a permanent impairment.

"I'm not going to get any better," they might say. "This is as good as I'm going to get. I don't want to go back to work at the construction company because my back is messed up. I'm 40 percent disabled." This claim may be supported by their treating doctor.

At that point, an investigator may be able to provide contradictory video evidence to the IME, QME, or AME (Independent Medical Evaluator, Qualified Medical Evaluator, or Agreed Medical Evaluator, respectively), who estimates the permanent impairment rating to be closer to 15 percent. This might also be time to do more surveillance in order to gather even more evidence. In some cases, however, the extent of disability is more obvious to an IME, QME, or AME—for example, if the injured worker is using a back brace or a cane during surveillance, and there is medical evidence to support the activity, which is consistent with their claim, surveillance may actually corroborate the claim.

The investigator's job is simply to arm the insurance company and employer with facts. For example, the investigator might say, "Based on six days of surveillance, the injured worker was not observed violating his or her lifting limitations," or, "The injured worker was observed violating his bending and stooping restriction while on an ATV guided mountain tour for six to eight hours."

You shouldn't hire an investigator to carry out surveillance for no specific reason. What is the purpose of the surveillance? What is the goal? Are you providing it to a doctor, a lawyer, a medical evaluator? Claims professionals must articulate a reasonable suspicion.

Ultimately, it's up to the insurance professional to know when, where, and how to use the right kind of investigation in a targeted way, with a specific goal in mind.

WHAT THE INVESTIGATOR NEEDS TO KNOW

Once an investigator is brought on board, they need to know as much as possible about the claim—every nuance and detail. Any information the employer and insurance adjuster can provide will help the investigation. Beyond basic information like height, weight, date of birth, and Social Security number, they need a recent photo ID, marital information, and anything that won't show up on a resume or job application. Do they have any kids? What kind of vehicle do they drive? The more information, the better.

Investigators also need to know when the claims examiner contacted the injured worker and if the worker is represented by a lawyer. If they don't yet have legal representation, then what conversation has already taken place? How difficult is it to get ahold of the injured worker? What have they already said about their current condition, both mentally and physically? If a doctor visit has already taken place, what are the most recent symptoms, complaints, and restrictions?

If the injured worker tells the claims examiner, "I used to go to the gym five days a week, but I can't do that anymore," that's important information to share with the investigator. Besides knowing as much as possible, the investigator needs to know what the goal is. In fact, knowing the specific goal is a critical part of the success of any investigation.

Once the goal is clear, investigators must have a clear sense of all federal, state, and local laws in regard to trespassing, privacy, chain of custody, and evidence, so they can make sure they act according to the law and in compliance with the fair claims practices contained in the Unfair Claims Settlement Practices Act. The goal is to always treat injured workers fairly, giving them the benefits they are entitled to. Investigators are committed to the same goal, ultimately, while also working to reduce costs and protect the insurance company and employer from further litigation.

If investigators bend the rules, fail to follow all laws regarding trespassing, privacy, or pretexting, or violate attorney-client privilege, they open themselves up to litigation. Since they work as an agent of the insurance company, they open up the insurance company and employer to litigation as well. Insurance companies and employers should never ask an investigator to do anything that falls outside the boundaries of the law.

WHAT THE EMPLOYER NEEDS TO KNOW

Employers need to understand best practices, which include the entire claims process, the impact of safety and prevention, and procedures for reporting and collecting evidence rapidly. When they see a red flag, they need to know what to do.

Worker Bob files a claim after an announcement is made by the employer that bonuses will not be paid out this year. His coworkers stand around the water cooler a week later and complain about their jobs. They express a desire for Bob to make the company pay. Someone overhears this conversation and warns management, "Bob is really going to get you guys because you didn't give any bonuses."

These kinds of scenarios reveal why management must keep an ear to the ground, listening for any clues as to worker motivation. Rather than sitting on that information, they should open a clear line of communication about it with investigators and potentially the claims examiner and at the minimum, report it to human resources for documentation purposes. Bob may also need closer supervision.

Large employers like Walmart and Boeing are self-insured, which means they have many of the same responsibilities as an insurance company depending on the state they are registered in. Fraudulent claims hit their bottom line directly. To become self-insured, states have vetting processes, so not every company qualifies, and the company may need five years of accredited financials and a certain amount of money in the bank based on the number of employees and prior loss ratios. All of this is set by state regulators.

SELF-INSURED EMPLOYERS

According to the State of California Department of Industrial Relations,[11] in 2016, 2.3 million California workers were covered by self-insurance, with a total of $100 billion in self-insured payroll. They also reveal that 3,134 California private entities are active self-insurers, with $4.8 billion in estimated claims reserves (EFL), $1.4 billion in medical and indemnity payments, and 85,563 open workers' compensation cases.

A warehouse worker at Nordstrom's files a claim, and it immediately becomes an indemnity claim because of the seriousness of the injury. Suppose a pallet fell off a truck and hit the worker on the head, neck, and shoulder. The person is so hurt, he literally can't show up the next day. Everyone in the area saw it happen, and the worker was bleeding. Now, he's going to miss three weeks of work as he recovers. From day one, the injury seems serious, so the company reserves $25,000 for this type of injury right away. The money is moved to a reserve account to pay for treatment, losses, and accommodations for the injured worker.

On day three, the worker gets out of the hospital, and he receives the first doctor's report: herniated disk, nine staples in his head, pain in the shoulder and hip. His

---

11   State of California Department of Industrial Relations. "Self-Insured Employers." https://www. dir.ca.gov/osip/SelfInsuredEmployers.htm (accessed May 14, 2018)

condition is worse than the company initially thought, so they reserve another $100,000 and move it to the reserve account.

Weeks go by, and the worker is not getting any better. He grows increasingly angry because he realizes his injury could have been prevented if his boss had taken proper precautions. Finally, the worker hires a lawyer.

"Don't worry about it," the lawyer says. "I'm going to get you a seven-figure payout."

When the examiner finds out about this, he can't believe it. He goes immediately to risk management. In good faith, the company has to increase the reserve account by a reasonable amount, based on preliminary MRI reports and X-rays. The company moves half a million dollars into the reserve account now.

Imagine a scenario where a large warehouse burns to the ground, and as a result of smoke inhalation, five hundred claims are filed. Every one of those claims will need a reserve of $10,000. As you might imagine, a self-insured employer often has their hands full trying to watch where every penny goes. This can cause a significant financial burden.

CASE STUDY

The following is an example highlighting the need for initiating an investigation as soon as any red flags are identified. A forty-three-year-old toolmaker allegedly sustained injuries to his spine, knees, and bilateral, lower extremities while employed by a mold and metal company.

Thomas Smith, president of the company, has been there since 1957. The injured worker is his own nephew and he's known him his entire life. However, they developed a business relationship as well when the injured worker began working for him in October 2015.

As a tool man, the injured worker mainly repaired and modified large metal molds, dismantling, repairing, and replacing components as needed. As part of his duties, he often machined new parts using a Computer Numeric Control (CNC) die-cutting machine, which is used in the prototyping and full production for cutting, carving, machining, and milling in materials like wood, medium-density fiberboard (MDF), plastics, foam, and aluminum.

To operate the machine, the injured worker placed the material he needed on the machine and input data to produce a particular component. Since he used a variety of tools to repair or manufacture parts, he was required to grind, weld, and polish many different components. According to Smith, the injured worker spent half of his time inputting data for the parts he needed. He also scanned the parts he wanted to replace.

The injured worker also happened to be the owner of a mold services company, though he wasn't successful at it, which is why Smith hired him. The injured worker didn't work forty hours a week at Smith's company. Instead, he came in whenever he wanted and submitted receipts and expense reports. On average, he worked around thirty-two hours a week.

Smith mentioned that he argued frequently with the injured worker. His nephew is irritable, and he often failed to communicate the status of specific jobs. Ultimately, his employment was terminated for misconduct. Specifically, the injured worker had an outburst in front of a client, behaving aggressively toward Smith and using foul language. The outburst occurred on April 10, 2017, and the injured worker left work early that day as a result. When Smith asked him to return, pick up his tools, and leave the key to the shop, the injured worker demanded to be paid for his sick time and vacation days. Even though there was reason to believe he had used all of his vacation days and sick leave, Smith decided to include it in the injured worker's final paycheck. They paid him, and his last day at the company was April 17, 2017.

At that time, Smith had no awareness of the injured worker's injury. The injured worker hadn't reported any injuries, pain, or discomfort to anyone, and he never complained about job duties causing any discomfort on the job. Smith never witnessed or heard about any incidents involving the injured worker that might have caused injury during his time of employment.

According to Smith, the injured worker participated in extreme sports such as skydiving, snowboarding, and skateboarding. In fact, the injured worker was a certified skydiver, though he had ceased skydiving after an accident. The injured worker went snowboarding approximately eight weeks prior to the date of his interview with Mr. Smith.

According to a coworker, Mrs. Villanueva, the injured worker often acted inappropriately with other employees. She recalled an incident where the injured worker became upset because she asked for expense receipts when he requested reimbursement. The injured worker didn't have any receipts and tried to convince Mrs. Villanueva that she should take his word for it.

After his termination, the injured worker filed a workers' comp claim for an injury that supposedly occurred during the six months of his employment. It appeared to be an act of retaliation. No one could corroborate his claims, and he never reported any injury until after he was fired.

The red flags in this case include:

- Disciplinary action precipitating a termination
- Post-termination workers' comp claim
- Lack of witnesses, evidence, or notification at the time of the injury
- The fact that the employer had procedures in place to identify, recognize, and report injuries, which the injured worker failed to do

The case was denied based on a lack of evidence and the fact that signs indicated that it was an attempt at retaliation. The post-termination claim prompted the claims examiner to hire an investigator to speak with human resources and other staff to see if anyone else could confirm the injured worker's account prior to termination. Since no one could corroborate his injuries, the company had grounds to deny the case. Even though the claim is denied, it can still be a costly claim if the injured worker continues to pursue through legal representation.

CHAPTER 4

TYPES OF CLAIMS

In 2003, as the Imola Avenue Bridge was being built to cross the Napa River, a hundred-foot section of the bridge collapsed without warning. The contracting company had both in-house and outsourced engineering, and a number of subcontractors provided work, so there were a large number of stakeholders. In a project like this, a number of regulatory bodies, including city planners and OSHA, provide oversight.

On the day of the accident, a large, hydraulic jack supporting the bridge structure slipped, sending eight steel beams and several tons of wood plunging seventy-five feet to the ground below. A twenty-year-old worker was buried beneath tons of debris and died. Three other workers on the eastern end of the collapsed portion of the bridge received injuries, as did four iron workers, who rode the collapse to the ground. Among the injured was a California Department of Transportation inspector who was overseeing the work on the $40 million bridge.

The project began as a replacement for the Maxwell Bridge, serving as part of a flood control project along the Napa River. The general contractor was C.C. Myers Construction of Rancho Cordova, and one of the subcontractors was Bay Area Rebar of San Francisco.

After the accident, the California Division of Occupational Safety and Health and California Department of Transportation (Caltrans) went to work to determine what happened and why. At the time, C.C. Myers happened to be a client of ours, as was Zurich Insurance, the insurance company that provided workers' compensation insurance for C.C. Myers employees. C.C. Myers also had a liability policy with another insurance carrier to cover the cost of repairs in the event of an accident.

Any contractor or subcontractor who worked for C.C. Myers—including the steel company and the hydraulic company—was also required to have workers' comp insurance and significant liability insurance to protect their own workers and cover any damages or loss they caused to the bridge project. In one case, a subcontractor had Zurich as their workers' comp insurance provider as well.

This created an incredibly complex situation. To further complicate matters, a number of workers, including the contractor, one subcontractor, and the government worker, sustained psychological injuries that weren't initially reported. A woman who was on the bridge that day later recounted the story of running for her life as the bridge collapsed under her feet. This experience produced PTSD.

Because of the complexity—involving both government and private workers, liability and workers' comp—every insurance company deployed its own legal counsel, and as part of deploying legal counsel, each one also hired their own investigators. The liability investigators worked to determine who was at fault and to what extent. On top of that, the government agencies, Caltrans and OSHA, did their own investigation to unravel what transpired and who was to blame.

In the end, many different investigators were involved, which meant victims and witnesses needed to be interviewed by a huge number of lawyers and investigators. OSHA and Caltrans took the lead on all interviewing of witnesses, appointing one person to ask the questions. The investigators were present for these interviews, listening and taking note of the details.

Ultimately, Caltrans had the authority to determine who

was at fault. It quickly turned into a fight between all of the insurance companies, as they tried to figure out how the blame would be divvied up. In a big case like this, no single person or entity generally takes 100 percent of the blame. Instead, the blame gets shared among multiple parties because of all the companies on the job site. For example, it was a subcontractor's job to make sure the brace didn't fall, but the inspector might have overlooked something. The manufacturing company that made the hydraulic lift also got dragged into the investigation because someone had to verify whether or not the jack was to blame. That meant the company that provided maintenance on the jack got involved as well.

During our investigation, we worked with all of the engineers to help us understand why the collapse occurred. Every insurance company wanted to hire their own engineers to determine what happened, so blame could be attributed fairly among all responsible parties. The shared risk in a case like this creates a tangled web.

At the same time, the government had a responsibility to the public to reveal how and why the accident happened and what it would cost to fix it. They also needed to make sure taxpayers didn't end up eating the cost.

These kinds of complex cases aren't rare. When a multi-car pileup happens on the freeway during a foggy afternoon, resulting in multiple injuries, it's difficult to determine who is at fault. It might take a year or more to sort it all out. In the meantime, the insurance company of every driver investigates every possible scenario to understand their share of the risk.

In the case of the Napa bridge collapse, insurance companies needed to investigate it thoroughly, digging deep and coordinating with investigators, accident reconstructionists, and lawyers to understand the facts. Ultimately, the truth can only be fully known with a thorough investigation.

MOST COMMON WORKERS' COMP CLAIMS

Workers' comp claims tend to fall into a handful of categories. These are the most common causes of on-the-job injuries:

OVEREXERTION

This happens when someone sustains an injury from something that puts a lot of stress on the body. This kind of injury can occur when, for example, a police officer tackles a suspect and wrenches his back, or when a convalescent nurse lifts a patient, grabs a rail in order to brace herself, and pulls a muscle.

SLIPS, TRIPS, AND FALLS

Slips occur from a wet or slick walking surface, which could be caused by rain, snow, grime, oil, wet leaves, or any number of things. Tripping occurs when someone catches their foot on something and falls. People often get injured as they catch themselves from a trip, and they end up breaking an ankle or straining their back. Falls often occur on rooftops, ladders, and stairs.

MACHINERY ACCIDENTS

Often, machine-related accidents are due to improper training or equipment that hasn't been properly maintained or operated safely. This might include a conveyor belt catching an appendage, a jackhammer crushing someone's foot, or a worker failing to wear eye goggles while operating a saw.

WORKPLACE VIOLENCE

According to the Bureau of Labor Statistics, nearly 400 people are shot on the job each year, and that's a low estimate. According to the FBI, the most dangerous job in America is as a convenience store worker. Robbery represents about 33 percent of workplace homicides, while coworker fights account for about 15 percent.

VEHICLE ACCIDENTS

Accidents are a common cause of workplace injuries for truck drivers, delivery drivers, and salespeople. A famous example occurred when a Walmart truck collided with comedian Tracy Morgan's limousine. In that incident, Morgan suffered a severe, traumatic brain injury on top of his orthopedic injuries. Often, the liability claims are paid for by a different insurance company than the workers' comp claim. However, at times, the employer may have the same insurance carrier for workers' compensation and liability.

STRUCK BY AN OBJECT

These kinds of injuries happen frequently in retail environments. Most often, it occurs when an object falls, striking someone on the way down.

REPETITIVE MOTION

This refers to cumulative trauma that develops from a worker doing the same activity over and over for a long period of time. For example, a worker in a paint factory might develop lung cancer from inhaling paint fumes after years of work. A stenographer might develop carpal tunnel syndrome after a thirty-year career. It could be a worker who develops tendonitis or bursitis from lifting heavy objects all day.

MEDICAL-ONLY CLAIMS VS. INDEMNITY

Medical-only claims are simple, first-aid issues or minor in nature, needing minimal medical treatment. A worker sprains her left wrist at work, goes to the doctor after work, takes some aspirin, and returns to work the next day. Since her job requires her right hand, she can resume her work right away. Maybe, to be safe, the supervisor gives her limited duty for a while. The insurance company pays for her treatment, and that's it.

Indemnity claims or lost-time claims happen when a worker is injured on the job and is unable to return to work unless and until the injury heals, has permanent impairment, and when the claim is being disputed by the employer. A construction worker injures her left arm to such a degree that she can never lift fifty pounds again. The company puts her to work operating a different piece of equipment, so she doesn't have to use that arm again. At that point, the injury is essentially permanent because it won't get any better. At best, the injury has reached maximum medical improvement (MMI).

PSYCHOLOGICAL INJURIES

Psychological injuries are common in accidents like the Napa bridge collapse but also in cases of workplace harassment. For example, a worker might be getting harassed by a supervisor to such a degree that the situation becomes violent. Maybe the supervisor is giving the worker bad shifts, calling them names, and purposely putting them at risk.

Perhaps, a woman working as a prison guard receives harassment and threats anytime she is posted in the yard by herself, but the supervisor keeps doing it anyway because he doesn't like her. This situation could easily become both a civil lawsuit and a workers' comp claim. Maybe the female worker goes to the doctor and says, "The situation at work is creating tremendous psychological stress."

Instances of sexual harassment can also result in both a civil lawsuit and workers' comp claim. An employee being harassed at work might tell the doctor, "I can't sleep. It's affecting my job performance. I need to take a month off work, and I need to see a therapist." These forms of harassment can also turn into indemnity claims.

It's common for a psychological claim to be added to an orthopedic claim. For example, a worker with a back injury has surgery and then starts taking medication. He feels depressed about life and puts on thirty pounds. In his marriage, he begins to have problems being intimate with his spouse, and this adds to the stress.

In all of these cases, an investigator needs to find out if

the claim is accurate. If a worker claims to have a psychological injury, the investigator should review the injured worker's claims, restrictions, limitations, and complaints, such as, "the worker sleeps all day, rarely goes outside, and no longer plays sports on the weekend."

Investigators will also want to check social media. Does the worker's Facebook profile tell a different story? Surveillance might be an option. It's important to get the injured worker on record, so they can state clearly what they can and can't do, how the injury is impacting their life, and why they can't return to work.

WHAT TYPES OF INJURIES ARE NOT COVERED?

Certain types of on-the-job injuries are not covered by workers' comp. Let's take a look at the major categories.

SELF-INFLICTED INJURIES

If a Wall Street banker leaps out of a window on the thirtieth floor, the injury won't be covered. Even though it happened at work, the incident had nothing to do with his actual duties. In a similar way, if workers get into a fight on the job, and the instigator gets punched in the face, the injury will not be covered. The worker who instigates the fight has no claim.

INJURIES WHILE THE WORKER WAS COMMITTING A CRIME

During an investigation into a workers' comp case in Oakland, we learned about a sanitation worker who doubled as a drug dealer. He routinely picked up his work truck, did actual sanitation work, then parked the vehicle, walked two blocks, stood on a corner, and hailed buyers. Since he was committing a crime, there's no way he would be covered for an injury. By the way, he was fired. Similarly, a worker who gets hurt while stealing from an employer will not be covered.

INJURIES THAT HAPPEN WHEN CONDUCT VIOLATES COMPANY POLICY

A salesperson works for a company with a no-drinking policy. One day, he goes to lunch with a client and gets inebriated. After lunch, he gets behind the wheel and causes a traffic accident. Since that's a violation of company policy, as well as a crime, the resulting injury would not be covered.

OTHER EXAMPLES

There are a number of scenarios in which a worker would not be covered in the event of an injury. If they are drunk or intoxicated on the job for any reason, they won't be covered. If they are horsing around at work, wrestling with another worker, and get injured, they probably won't be covered. Also, injuries that don't happen on the job aren't covered.

CASE STUDY

A twenty-three-year-old worker at a San Francisco restaurant got into an argument with his supervisor about the section of the restaurant he was assigned because it didn't get as much volume. He was a skinny young man named Charlie, who was a frequent marijuana smoker. The better section was given to a kid who had been a football player at Stanford. He was still in college, though he no longer played football. The two workers got into an argument during work, and the supervisor took the side of the former football player.

The skinny worker pushed the much bigger worker. That set off the former football player, who punched Charlie, dragged him across a dining table, and threw him into a glass memorabilia case. That caused Charlie to split his head open, requiring thirty staples.

A claim was filed. When we investigated, all we knew initially was that a fight had taken place. We didn't know who started it, but we knew we needed to get to the bottom of it. After all, fist fights are not a normal part of being a waiter, and not a typical cause of injury on the job.

We visited the injured worker in the hospital and spoke with him. Then we spoke with the supervisor and a nurse who happened to be at the restaurant the day of the fight. We learned the reason why the injured worker was upset, and we also learned that he'd showed up to work that day under the influence of marijuana—in clearing out his hospital locker, the employer found marijuana. Through interviews, we learned that the injured worker acted as the aggressor. Due to these circumstances, the worker's claim was denied.

After a month, the injured worker was sent to a county hospital. By this point, he had accrued $30,000 in medical bills, and the insurance company refused to cover any of it because he was the aggressor. We met with him again at this point, and he still had staples in his head. The hospital had intended to remove them two weeks after the fight, but because he had no insurance, he'd had to wait for the county to approve payment for the procedure.

By that point, he'd had staples in his head so long that his scalp had grown over them. The insurance company had made the decision not to pay for anything, so he hired a lawyer and sued. The lawsuit dragged on for two years.

Just because a claim gets denied doesn't mean it's over. However, for those two years, the injured worker received nothing. The lawyer argued that even though his client started the fight, the other worker had used excessive force. Despite the circumstances of the injury, the insurance company knew that judges are human. A judge might see the severity of the worker's injury and take pity on him. The former football player, after all, didn't get hurt.

To avoid a possible ruling in favor of the injured worker, the insurance company settled the case for $36,000.

In the end, the investigation almost certainly saved the insurance company a lot of money by providing a strong enough defense to reduce the size of the settlement. Remember, it's not just about getting a fraud conviction or restitution. Ultimately, a claim investigation can be used to help reduce the overall cost and risk for the insurance company.

CHAPTER 5

CASE LAW

The term "pretexting" refers to any circumstance in which an investigator poses as someone he is not. State laws on the legality of pretexting vary. In California, the law expressly allows pretexting when an investigator is investigating allegations of insurance fraud. The legality of the technique depends on circumstances, chiefly the objective of the pretext and who the investigator pretends to be.

It's always unlawful to pose as a law enforcement officer or a government employee such as a postal worker, firefighter, or utility company worker. The list of prohibited impersonations is long but should always be consulted before assuming an identity. Posing as a private delivery service employee is permitted, but even when the impersonation is permitted, the investigator can't trick someone into giving consent that would otherwise be considered trespassing or an invasion of privacy.

Laws governing audio recording are very strict and carry significant penalties for violations. Telephone conversations should never be recorded unless the consent of every party in the conversation is obtained in advance. It's a common misconception that one spouse can give consent to have a telephone recording device attached to a home phone. Simply because one spouse has legal access to a phone does not mean he can secretly record conversations on it.

Likewise, an investigator cannot assist someone in making a secret recording, even if the investigator does not listen in. Audio recordings using parabolic microphones or similar enhanced listening devices should never be made. With a few exceptions, such recordings will be declared an invasion of privacy, which will subject the responsible party to civil and criminal penalties.

Eavesdropping is also a violation of the law, even if the conversation is not recorded. One area of ongoing debate is whether a private investigator, who has identified himself, can secretly record a witness interview. Because of the debate and uncertainty, at Apex, our policy prohibits the recording of witnesses without documented consent.

VIDEO RECORDING

Surreptitious video recordings carry significantly less risk than surreptitious audio recordings. The essential question is whether or not the subject of the video recording had a reasonable expectation of privacy. Determining factors include the location of the subject at the time of recording, as well as the location of the camera. If the subject was readily visible to passersby or the public, even while on his own property, then it's lawful.

Video recordings of people engaged in sexual activity, or undressed, must be avoided. Whether or not an investigator can secretly video through the window of a home remains a gray area, even if the investigator is lawfully positioned. At Apex, we avoid any recording or photography that falls within the gray area. We don't videotape injured workers inside medical office waiting areas. While this may be considered a public area, videotaping a waiting room still falls within the gray area because of possible privacy concerns.

TRESPASSING, STALKING, AND HARASSMENT

Physical surveillance often includes the use of visual aids, such as binoculars and cameras. However, even surveillance that does not include electronic devices can result in violation of the law. The most common pitfalls are trespassing, stalking, and harassment.

Stalking and harassment are similar, but not identical. Stalking refers to the willful, malicious, and repeated following of someone, which creates a credible fear for that person's safety or the safety of their family. Harassment is a course of conduct directed at a specific person, which seriously alarms, annoys, torments, or terrorizes that person, and which serves no legitimate purpose.

An investigation conducted by a licensed investigator is considered a legitimate purpose, and in a carefully conducted surveillance, the subject has no idea he or she is being watched. Hence, that person cannot claim to be a stalking or harassment victim. However, if the investigator suspects the subject has become aware of the surveillance, the surveillance should be terminated immediately and reported to the licensee. This is considered a best practice, since it protects the legitimacy of the investigation.

Trespassing is a misdemeanor, defined as entering the property of another person without the owner or tenant's consent. Though easy to state, it is often tricky to apply. Many residents have sidewalks leading to a front porch or door. It is generally not trespassing to walk uninvited onto private property via the sidewalk, even to stand on the porch and knock on the door. This concept is called "implied consent" and means that, lacking a clear warning to the contrary, visitors, salesmen, mail carriers, delivery companies, and others are permitted to enter private property without trespassing. The mere presence of a fence or unlocked gate does not negate implied consent. After all, many homeowners have fences for decorative reasons or to keep pets and small children from wandering off.

ACTIONS TO AVOID

The investigator's job is to objectively document an injured worker's activity and gather relevant information about them. Opinions or suppositions are to be avoided. Investigators can pretext to find out information on the injured worker by phone or at the injured worker's or a neighbor's front door, but they must never pretext prior to receiving authorization from the client. Every request for a pretext should be evaluated individually.

The following actions should be absolutely avoided for legal reasons:

- Investigators should never obtain video at funerals, weddings, church services, or any activity that would be considered personal or private in nature, since this would be a violation of the injured worker's right to privacy. Plenty of case law has settled this issue, precluding any such activity.
- Investigators can't climb trees to obtain video over a privacy fence. They can't stand on ladders to obtain

a view not afforded to the general public. They can't remove or cut shrubbery to obtain an enhanced view. They can't peer through slats or knotholes in a fence. A subject can be videotaped using an ATM, but not while conducting a transaction, and investigators cannot obtain their PIN.

GATED COMMUNITIES

Gated communities are considered private property. If the gate leading into the neighborhood is closed, requires a passkey, or has a guard posted, then the investigator can't enter the property by foot unless foot traffic is not restricted. The investigator can't enter property where signs restrict access. In this situation, using a pretext to gain consent to enter is considered trespassing.

The only exception is when the investigator has lawful access to a gated community. In that case, videotaping is permissible as long as the investigator remains on communal property such as a public street and doesn't record nonpublic activities.

INDIAN CASINOS

Casinos are owned either by a tribe or a private corporation. As long as they are open to the public, anyone may enter. However, the owner has the authority to ask an invited guest to leave if they are engaging in unapproved activity.

Whether videotaping is expressly prohibited is determined on a case-by-case basis. Secretly videotaping in violation of a posted policy is not a crime and does not by itself subject the taping party to civil action, but videotaping must be restricted to actions that aren't private. For example, filming someone gambling in an open area where others are present and watching is acceptable, but filming inside a restroom is not. Bear in mind, surreptitious audiotaping is never allowed.

GOLF COURSES

At golf courses, it is permissible to videotape a subject who is playing because no one has an expectation of privacy on a golf course. However, trespassing to gain visual access to the subject is prohibited even if the course is public. To get around this, the investigator will have to pay greens fees, so they can access the course legally.

TELEPHONE PRETEXTING

Using a telephone to pretext is fundamentally no different from any other kind of pretexting. If used to acquire private information, it constitutes an invasion of privacy. On the other hand, if pretexting is used to simply confirm if the subject resides at a particular residence, it is generally acceptable. However, the investigator cannot impersonate a government official or any of the occupations listed in the Business and Professions Code.[12]

DELIVERY PRETEXTING

If the investigator creates a fake company or employee status to gain access to otherwise private property, obtain private information, or gain access to a vantage point from which to videotape the subject, these would be considered trespassing. Unfortunately, city and county employers, even lawyers, in many cases ask workers' comp investigators to do these kinds of activities.

DRONE SURVEILLANCE

Laws regulating the use of drones during investigations are fairly new. If an investigator wants to conduct surveillance on a private golf course, they might be tempted to circumvent privacy laws by using a drone to fly over the golf course. However, recent laws have established that this is trespassing. In general, avoiding drone use altogether is considered a best practice.

---

12 California State Legislature. "Business and Professions Code." California Legislative Information. https://leginfo.legislature.ca.gov/faces/codesTOCSelected.xhtml?tocCode=BPC (accessed on May 8, 2018)

To gain a clearer sense of the laws regarding privacy issues, we spoke with David Queen, a lawyer who has written policy on these issues for Apex. He can speak clearly to the best practices regarding some of the legal complexities affecting workers' comp investigations.

INSIGHTS FROM DAVID QUEEN, ESQ.

In the state of California, issues of privacy are dealt with in Article 1, Section 1 of the California Constitution, which specifically declares that privacy is an "inalienable right." Numerous statutes have been designed to enforce and clarify that right.

When investigating insurance fraud, a statutory exemption allows insurance fraud investigators to engage in pretexting in a way that does not apply to a typical private investigator. However, I always tell private investigators that if something is legal, they should consider what impact it will make on a jury. If the investigator's behavior appears to be in bad taste, it might influence a jury in the wrong direction.

The two primary issues that influence surveillance are trespassing and invasion of privacy. An investigator should always begin with a key question: am I trespassing? Any form of trespassing can lead to Bureau of Security and Investigative Services (BSIS) discipline, up to and including revocation of license. Gaining consent to enter a property under false pretenses invalidates consent and becomes trespassing. An investigator can't lie to a subject to gain entry into a house.

The second key question that an investigator should ask is, "Am I engaged in an invasion of privacy?" Some people confuse surveillance with videotaping, either conflating the two or artificially separating them.

Surveillance in a public park is perfectly acceptable, whatever activity is taking place. The law draws no distinction between activities. An open-air baptism is not considered a private activity, even though it's a religious event. Neither is public prayer. If the subject later says, "I was praying, so the investigator invaded my privacy," that wouldn't be a valid accusation.

On the other hand, sometimes investigators invade a subject's privacy and defend the activity by saying, "I only watched; I didn't videotape anything." However, the operative activity isn't videotaping. Whether or not the investigator records the surveillance is not the deciding factor.

Almost no investigators today conduct surveillance without documenting what they observe. They document partly to protect themselves, so they can't be accused of lying. These days, clients, juries, and judges expect documentation for everything, so anytime an investigator conducts surveillance, regardless of the activity taking place—a wedding, a baptism on the beach, a pool party—they might as well bring a camera. Having a camera won't increase the likelihood of being sued for invasion of privacy.

The test for whether or not an activity is an invasion of privacy comes down to a single issue: does the subject have a reasonable expectation of privacy 100 percent of the time? For example, although prayer, along with religious activity in general, is protected, the expectation of privacy doesn't extend to public prayer. It's no different than doing tai chi exercises in public.

What if an investigator uses binoculars to see through a living room window? The subject has left the curtains open, and he is observed to be engaged in physical activity inconsistent with his claimed injury. After a moment, the subject walks out of view of the binoculars, and when he returns, he's naked. He has no idea he's being watched, and the investigator has no camera.

When the subject finds out and claims that their privacy was invaded, the investigator might be tempted to respond by pointing out that they didn't record anything. That defense won't work, although if it was videotaped, it might increase the damages by making the humiliation worse. Again, the determining factor is whether or not the subject had a reasonable expectation of privacy.

Some investigations get highly intrusive, so it's very important for investigators to fully understand the risks involved in surveillance. Anything that might be trespassing, stalking, harassment, or an invasion of privacy should be avoided.

Trespassing means entering private property without the consent of the owner. Invasion of privacy simply means the subject has a reasonable expectation of privacy in a certain location.

A REASONABLE EXPECTATION OF PRIVACY

An investigator is conducting an insurance fraud investigation on a worker who claims to have badly injured her back. According to the worker, she can no longer bend at the waist or lift heavy objects. The investigator sets up surveillance cater-corner to the house and observes the worker walking around on her property, engaging in physical activity inconsistent with the claimed injury.

Upon learning about the surveillance later, the injured worker says it was an invasion of privacy. Is she right? No, because she was in a location where anyone driving down the street or walking down the sidewalk could easily observe her. The fact that the activity itself was private doesn't matter.

What if the subject had gone inside the house but left the living room curtains open? In that case, the law says she had no reasonable expectation of privacy because she exposed her activity to anybody passing by.

An investigator does not need any probable cause to conduct surveillance. Even an average person can follow anyone else as long as they don't do it in a harassing or stalking manner. The investigator doesn't have to wait until he suspects the subject of wrongdoing. A suspicion alone is enough. The investigation might prove those suspicions true or disprove them.

When dealing with issues of privacy, the law uses the standard "reasonable." A lawyer might claim, "My client is a very private person. Just the thought of somebody watching her has caused great emotional trauma," but the law doesn't care about the subjective feelings of the client. Instead, the law looks at what a "reasonable" person would feel. A reasonable person doesn't experience "great emotional trauma" from an investigator watching them mow the lawn.

Of course, that doesn't take into account how a jury will

react. With a jury, twelve people are applying their own individual, half-baked ideas of what "reasonable" means. That's why judges often have to remind juries that their personal views aren't relevant.

A specific jurist might feel that it's rude to videotape someone praying in a public park, but it doesn't matter. A reasonable person engaging in that activity in public would not feel invaded because someone observed them doing it.

This is why paparazzi are still able to operate legally. When Jennifer Aniston goes out to dinner, the paparazzi can photograph her as much as they want, even if she personally feels invaded. However, if someone climbs a tree to look over her walled backyard and takes photos of her sunbathing nude, it becomes a legal problem. Why? Because a reasonable person expects to have privacy behind the walls of their own home.

Ultimately, in determining whether or not an invasion of privacy has taken place, three things must be taken into account: the location of the observer, the location of the person being observed, and the activity of the person being observed. By taking these three things into consideration and applying a bit of common sense, the legality of the situation can be readily determined.

GETTING AHEAD OF THE LAW

Drones are an example of technology getting ahead of the law. When the California Constitution was written, lawmakers didn't anticipate the kinds of electronic contraptions that future generations would have to deal with.

In California, common law—also called case law—interprets statutes, in many cases creating privacy rights not expressly written in the Constitution. In other cases, specific statutes have been written to deal with issues related to new technology, among them wiretap laws.

Case law is clear that investigators are allowed to electronically enhance video. That's why telephoto lenses and binoculars are permitted. If an investigator can't see the subject from a hundred feet away and takes out a pair of binoculars to get a better view, that's perfectly acceptable.

In regard to audio, the laws are much stricter. If the subject is meeting with someone at a restaurant, and the investigator can hear every word from a nearby table, he can hit "record" on his iPhone and set it on the table. That's also permissible. On the other hand, I strongly discourage private investigators from using parabolic microphones because of the strict nature of audio recording laws.

Infrared cameras can also be problematic. If the subject drives to a secluded location, and the investigator can only see a silhouette in the car, it might be tempting to take out the infrared camera. Now, at least, they can read the license plate and get a clear sense of what the subject is doing.

The risk is that the subject will claim the investigator went too far, and the legal situation isn't always clear. The investigator's defense might be, "I saw the subject get into that car with that license plate, and he never stopped until he parked in a secluded location."

If it was broad daylight, and he could see the car clearly and read the license plate, it wouldn't be a problem. Even if he whipped out a telephoto lens to take a close picture, it's fine. If he pulled out a parabolic microphone and started recording, then the investigator has a problem. The legal theory is that he can see the subject with the unaided eye, but he cannot hear inside the car with an unaided ear. A telescopic lens only enhances what can already be seen, but a parabolic microphone provides a capability that he would not otherwise possess.

What makes all of this more complex is that there are multiple legal theories for the same set of facts. A judge may decide to toss out one theory and leave another in place. In some instances, all of the theories apply.

In other words, one set of facts can result in multiple torts.

An intrusive investigation might be an invasion of privacy, or it could be trespassing. Then again, it might be both, and on top of that, the judge might decide it's a stalking and harassment case as well.

AN UNREASONABLY INTRUSIVE INVESTIGATION

According to the court ruling in *Noble v. Sears & Roebuck*, "An unreasonably intrusive investigation may violate a plaintiff's right to privacy."

This case provides a clear example of what an intrusive investigation looks like, and it's a case law that still gets cited today, even though it's almost forty years old. It was a tricky case because the behavior of the investigator went just a little too far but didn't fit the standard definition of trespassing or invasion of privacy.

Complicating matters, the court didn't discuss the facts of the case in great detail. They ruled that the investigator pretexted his way into a hospital room, but they never specified how he did it. Consequently, when we read the court documents years later, we have no idea if he lied to a nurse, claimed to be the patient's uncle, or used some other method. We don't know what he said. All we know is the investigator somehow gained access to the patient's hospital room.

In this case, Noble was the name of a woman who had been injured while on a shopping trip at a Sears store. Sears hired an investigator to locate a man who had supposedly accompanied her on that trip. Why the company didn't simply wait for a deposition is unclear.

According to the court records, "[Sears] hired a PI to locate the man who had been with her. In order to secure his address from the injured woman, the investigator gained admittance to the hospital room where she was confined, and by deception secured the address." This formed the basis for Noble to claim an invasion of privacy, since she has exclusive right of occupancy in her hospital room. The court ultimately ruled in her favor.

In a similar case, *Redner v. Workers' Comp*, the investigator befriended the injured person and convinced her to go horseback riding. During the horseback ride, the investigator had the woman videotaped in order to prove she wasn't injured. Since he lied to get her to participate in the activity, the court ruled that it was an intrusive investigation.

There's a principle in the law called "fraud in the inducement." If someone entices you to buy a piece of land in Arizona by claiming that it's sitting on top of oil, but you discover, after buying it, that there's no oil, that's an example of fraud in the inducement. That was the accusation against the investigator in *Redner v. Workers' Comp*. However, the court also ruled that the investigator should not profit from his own deceitful conduct. Even though that ruling doesn't point to a specific statute on the book, the court was applying what they considered common sense in regard to fairness and good conduct.

One thing I always tell investigators is, "When in doubt, ask yourself, 'Will this pass the smell test?'" To put it another way, "What would my grandmother think if she was sitting on the jury and found out what I'd done to gain access to the subject?" In other words, it might seem technically legal because it doesn't break a specific statute, but you'll have a hard time defending it in court.

MORE CASE LAW EXAMPLES

In the case *Unruh v. Truck Insurance*, the court referred back to the Redner case, writing, "The high purpose of the worker compensation laws should not be perverted by resorting to evidence perfidiously procured. Our condemnation in the Redner case leaves no doubt that such conduct goes beyond the normal role of an insurer and a compensation scheme intended to protect the worker." The investigator in *Unruh v. Truck Insurance* had befriended the victim and talked her into going to Disneyland. He then videotaped her climbing onto rides to prove she was not as injured as she claimed.

Another relevant case is *Academy of Motion Picture Arts*

and Sciences v. Olsen, in which the Academy learned that tickets were being scalped for the Oscars. They hired an investigator, who posed as a buyer interested in purchasing scalped tickets. In this instance, the court had no problem with the investigator's lie. What this indicates is that courts are generally more vigilant when it comes to intrusive investigations in workers' comp cases.

Unfortunately, although no judge or jury would admit this, sometimes the distinction is made because of emotion. Courts have more compassion for cases involving personal injury and workers' comp, even in the face of potential fraud, so companies have to be more vigilant during investigations.

The courts ruled against the investigators in these cases, even though there's a statute specifically allowing investigators to pretext in instances where there's a reasonable suspicion of insurance fraud. My advice to investigators on a workers' comp case is to document everything and always ask supervisors before carrying out any pretexting activities.

ESTABLISH A REASONABLE SUSPICION

In one case, a worker filed a claim stating that he could no longer work because of a serious on-the-job injury. A private investigator followed him, and according to his surveillance logs, the worker routinely went into an auto parts store and stayed there for hours at a time. Because of this, the insurance company suspected him of insurance fraud, but they were unsure of how to proceed.

At that point in an investigation, the question for investigators becomes, "How can I get physically closer to the suspect?"

Before doing any pretexting, it is vitally important to document the reasonable suspicion against the worker. Having done that, let's suppose the investigator pretends to be a salesman at the auto parts shop. The worker shows up and asks for a muffler, and the investigator goes into the back to retrieve it.

In this instance, the pretexting would be allowed because a reasonable suspicion of fraud has been identified and documented beforehand. The trick is that "investigator dishonesty" is often used as a basis for revoking a license. This creates many of the gray areas that make investigations such a challenge. The safest course is to always act cautiously and only in the face of clear facts.

If all pretexting was prohibited, there would be a bright-line test. Process servers lie all the time, as do bounty hunters, and they are legally allowed to do so. However, in the case of investigators, it depends on the situation and the extent of the pretexting.

During a recent California Association of Licensed Investigators (CALI) Conference in Reno, after giving a speech on pretexting, a member of the audience came up to me afterward and pulled a picture of a small, fluffy dog out of his pocket.

"I carry this with me everywhere," he said.

"So, you're a dog lover?" I replied.

"No, I don't have a dog. Actually, I can't stand them. I use this photo anytime I'm conducting surveillance at a house when I'm not sure if anybody's home, especially when the client is cost sensitive. I don't want to surveil an empty house, so I knock on the front door. If nobody answers, chances are good that nobody's home and I break off the surveillance. However, if somebody comes to the door, I whip out the picture and say, 'Hi, my mom lives just around the corner. She's elderly and her little dog Fufu ran off. Have you seen her? There's a twenty-dollar reward.'"

That's an example of harmless pretexting. Courts will never turn on an investigator for that kind of tactic.

DEGREES OF DISHONESTY

The case law about pretexting is all about degrees of

dishonesty. Pretexting by its very nature is a form of dishonesty, but the pretext about Fufu the dog doesn't hurt anyone. It's not the same as lying to get into someone's private hospital room. In *Noble v. Sears & Roebuck*, the investigator might have saved the case by presenting documentation of the evidence that showed a reasonable suspicion that Noble was engaged in insurance fraud.

Even then, Noble's lawyer could have responded, "The level of pretexting was impermissible because it crossed a threshold by entering a hospital room where the patient had medical charts hanging on the edge of the bed." Nobody can predict how the court will respond, even in the face of a reasonable suspicion. That's why I always tell clients, "The gray area is huge. Proceed at your own risk."

ENTRAPMENT

How does an intrusive investigation relate to entrapment? When most people hear the term "entrapment," they assume it has something to do with tempting people to commit a crime. For example, they imagine a case where an undercover narcotics agent approaches a suspect and says, "I've got some fabulous Afghani heroin with fentanyl mixed in. It's 100 percent pure. I'll knock 30 percent off the price if you buy today." If the suspect agrees, law enforcement swoops in and arrests him.

That's not entrapment. Entrapment is when a suspect is induced through indefensible means to engage in conduct they would not otherwise have engaged in. Offering to sell drugs doesn't fall into that category. On the other hand, if the agent continues to offer drugs to the point of harassment over a long period of time, using all kinds of enticements, threats, and promises, then a court might consider it entrapment.

In the case of *Redner v. Workers' Comp*, the female suspect was smitten with the attractive male investigator. He suggested they go horseback riding together, and she agreed. He didn't have to keep pushing over a long period of time, so it's not considered entrapment. However, it was still determined to be an intrusive investigation.

The danger with workers' comp investigations is rarely entrapment. The actionable tort is the intrusive investigation. However, even when conduct falls short of being an actionable tort, the California Bureau of Security and Investigative Services can still pull someone's license over their own rules regarding "dishonesty."

I liken it to the military's provision in the Court Martial Code called "conduct unbecoming an officer." This is used as a catchall term anytime the court can't figure out how else to go after someone. These issues are often in the eye of the beholder. Like that famous comment regarding pornography, "I may not be able to define it, but I know it when I see it." In the same way, in regard to workers' comp investigations, courts will sometimes say, "This pretexting was so transparently offensive that it becomes an intrusive investigation."

In the case of the investigator entering a private hospital room, this decision is understandable. Clearly, it was a case of intruding into someone's privacy. However, inviting a suspect to Disneyland or horseback riding doesn't seem particularly intrusive. In both cases, the investigators were able to provide evidence of fraud as a result of the pretexting, even if the pretexting was somewhat unsavory.

What's the point? Investigators must pursue the facts very carefully and diligently. In investigations, 95 percent of the calls I receive are about privacy, intrusive investigations, and pretexting. I always tell people to be wary of crossing any lines of good taste or decency.

DRONE USAGE IN INVESTIGATIONS

Drones are incredibly easy to operate, and the more expensive models have high-definition cameras with sophisticated zoom capability. FAA rules for radio-controlled aircraft state that they cannot exceed 400 feet in altitude and can't operate near airports or heavily populated areas, like Dodger Stadium during a baseball game. These are strictly intended as safety rules.

For investigative work, according to current law, drones must be registered with the FAA, which gives the drone a specific serial number. That serial number must be placed on the drone, so if it crashes, they can trace it back to its owner.

Flying a drone for commercial reasons also requires obtaining a UAV license, though this is not difficult. Specific information about acquiring the license can be obtained at www.faa.gov/uas. There's a written test, but online courses can help. Operating a drone for any commercial reason without a license can result in a hefty fine, so I strongly discourage investigators from doing it.

Assuming a drone is registered and the operator is licensed, what are the rules governing drone usage during a workers' comp investigation? In California, a law (AB-856) went into effect in January 2017 suggesting that an investigator cannot park a drone over private property in order to watch someone. This was actually intended as an anti-paparazzi measure, but it extends to anyone using a drone.

State Senate bill SB-142 extends liability for wrongful occupation of real property and damages to any person who operates an unmanned aircraft system within the air space over real property (defined as less than 350 feet above ground level) without express permission from the property owner. Among other things, this tightens restrictions on the types of activity that can be legally recorded on private property.

Often, investigators need to use drones in rural areas where it's hard to set up surveillance without being spotted. To do this, they might approach a neighbor, so they can fly a drone above the neighbor's property in order to get a clear view of the suspect on the adjacent property.

This is similar to a case where the investigator rented a second-floor bedroom at a neighbor's house so he could look into the suspect's property. When he did that, he caught the suspect engaged in all manner of rigorous activity. The suspect sued for invasion of privacy, but the case was tossed out.

The reason the investigator didn't get in trouble in that case is because he didn't scale a wall and had permission from the property owner to be in that second-floor bedroom. The neighbor had a clear view into the suspect's property all the time, so there was no legal problem with allowing a third party to do so.

Unfortunately, with the new law in California, there isn't yet enough case law to know how it will be applied. It's possible that investigators in California will no longer be able to use these kinds of tactics, particularly if they use a drone to see over a fence. Then again, I believe this law is unconstitutional, so it might end up getting contested. Also, it seems clear that FAA regulations should trump state laws.

My advice to investigators wanting to obtain footage using a drone is threefold. First, make sure you have the proper license. Second, make sure you have permission from the property owner where you want to fly the drone. Third, make sure the suspect is participating in activity that you can legally observe. If you're watching them sunbathe, you're operating in a gray area. A year ago, this might have been legal, but recent laws have tightened restrictions.

We simply don't know for sure how juries are going to apply these new laws. Which actions will they perceive as violating the anti-paparazzi laws? How will they apply these laws in defining intrusive investigations? Time will tell.

PHYSICAL INVASION OF PRIVACY VS. CONSTRUCTIVE INVASION OF PRIVACY

Adding to the complexity, there's a distinction between a physical invasion of privacy and a constructive invasion of privacy, just as there's a difference between actual possession of narcotics and constructive possession of narcotics. If you've ever watched an episode of *Cops*, you know what happens when someone gets pulled over. If the cop perceives that the driver is acting a little "out there," he will make the driver get out of the vehicle. He will check his pupils to see if they're dilated, and then he will pat him down. If he finds drugs in his pocket, that's actual possession of narcotics. If he then searches the trunk and finds more drugs, that's constructive possession of narcotics.

Physical invasion of privacy requires intruding into someone's private space, whereas constructive invasion of privacy is more about the attempt. Though it's a simplification, according to California Civil Code 1708.8(a), a person is liable for physical invasion of privacy when knowingly entering private property without permission or invading the privacy of the plaintiff with intent to capture a visual image or sound recording of the person engaged in a personal or familial activity. However, it's constructive invasion of privacy when they attempt to capture an image, video, or sound recording in a manner that is offensive to a reasonable person, regardless of whether or not physical trespassing takes place.

An investigator can't use failure as a defense. "Yes, I attempted to trespass, but I failed, so I didn't actually trespass." Remember, everyone is afforded the right to a reasonable expectation of privacy. The usage of a piece of technology in a way that would extend an individual's vantage point beyond what would be available to a neighbor, passerby, or the general public constitutes a violation of privacy.

CHAPTER 6

CLAIMS INVESTIGATIONS

Let's look at what's involved in a claims investigation. The first and perhaps most important step is the interview process. The injured worker will be asked a range of questions covering their current injuries, complaints, and limitations. Since the injury is driving the claim, that will be the focus. At the beginning of any interview with witnesses, employers, and injured workers, the investigator must request permission to record their statements. Once permission is given, the investigator must make the same permission request while recording their affirmative response. Photographs of witnesses or the injured workers must be done the same way.

The first and most basic question is to ask the injured worker's name. After that, questions will begin probing deeper into the worker's identity.

"Have you ever received medical treatment under a different name? Have you ever been married? Have you ever changed your name for any reason other than marriage? Are you an immigrant? If so, did you change your name when you arrived in the United States?

It's also important to obtain information about where the subject lives and how they can be contacted.

"Where do you live? How do we contact you? Do you live in an apartment? A condo? Are there stairs? Is there an elevator? Do you own, or do you rent?"

This information could have an impact later on if the investigator ends up conducting surveillance. Along with contact information, it's important to find out if the subject plans on moving. Also, their Social Security number and driver's license should be verified to make sure they are who they say they are. Marital status and family situation need to be covered, including any children, stepchildren, or adopted children.

Children can play a role in a subject's motivation to file a claim. If they lack childcare, it might seem easier and more lucrative to file a workers' comp claim, receive part of their salary, and save on childcare expenses by staying off work.

Information about gender, height, weight, and any distinguishing features can help with future identification for surveillance purposes. Background checks should be conducted to identify or verify prior injuries, prior treatment, gym membership, business ownership, as well as social media public profiles.

It's a good practice for investigators to make notes about household activities. They should get photographs of the injured worker and their injuries, noting their body language. For example, did the subject seem to be in pain? Does it appear consistent with their declared level of pain? Any photos on their desk or wall can also serve as clues.

EMPLOYMENT INFORMATION

Once all basic information has been gathered about the injured worker's identity and health, it's time to delve into their employment history.

"How long have you worked here? What do you do in your position? Have you had any human resource problems? What are your current job duties? Can you return to work? If not, why not?"

It's important to determine whether or not their restrictions prevent them from going back to work, so the next line of questioning will paint a picture of how each task is performed.

"Please, take me through a typical day, starting with your arrival at work and ending with your final task. How often do you sit and stand each day? Do you use any safety equipment? Do you buy this equipment yourself, or is it provided by the company? How much do you lift? How often? How repetitive is your work? If you do mostly computer work, have you ever been given an ergonomic evaluation?"

"Who are your supervisors? How long have the supervisors worked there? How many days a week? Are there any direct supervisors for your specific job duties? Have they had any incidents at that particular job? How many days a week do you work? What days of the week do you work? Do you work overtime? Are you in a union? If so, which one? Do you have a second job? Any supplemental employment?"

Questioning will delve into the entire past employment history of the subject. The same questions asked about the current job will be directed at each past job. After all employment has been addressed, questions will turn to other forms of income. Possible sources of income include the following: dividends, alimony, child support, court awards, unemployment compensation, capital gains, pensions, annuities, lump sum distributions, retirement plans, vacation property income, clergy income, gambling income, scholarships, a 401(k) plan, or passive stock options.

Military history should also be covered.

"Were you in the military? Was it active duty, or was it reservist? When did you enlist? Where were you stationed? What was your rank? What did you do? Were you ever injured? Did you receive a discharge? If so, what type?"

The reason for the thorough nature of the questioning is that the answers can provide numerous clues. For example, if the person earns money part time as a clergy member, but suddenly, post-injury, they've decided to take on a full-time role, that's something to take note of.

DESCRIPTION OF THE INCIDENT

Finally, questions will turn to an actual description of the injury. An extensive examination of when and how the accident occurred will be vital to the investigation. This begins by clarifying what the subject was doing prior to the incident.

"Did you work on the day prior to the injury? Where did

you work? What did you do? Did you participate in any physical activities the day before the injury? Did you play any sports in the days prior to the incident? Did you sustain an injury or experience any pain or discomfort from playing sports?"

Gradually, the questions walk the subject through exactly what happened on the day of the injury.

"What time did you wake up the day of the incident? Where were you when the injury happened?"

From this point on, the goal is to obtain a detailed, step-by-step explanation. Anything related to the mechanics and environment must be touched on. The who, what, where, when, and how must all be fully covered.

"Were there any witnesses? What are their names and titles? Do you work there still? Are there any surveillance cameras in the area? How far was the closest person working from you at the time of the incident? When the incident occurred, did you make any expressions of pain or discomfort, like yelling, crying, hitting something, or throwing something?"

After fully exploring the accident itself, the questions will cover everything that happened afterward.

"After the incident, did you stop working or resume normal

activities? Did you report or complain about the injury to anyone on the day of the injury? If not, why not? When did you report it? What did that person instruct you to do? Did you finish the rest of your shift or leave work early? Could you work without any restrictions? If not, please describe how you continued to work. Did your supervisor give you modified duties, or did you modify your duties yourself? If you went home, how did you get there? What did you do when you got home?"

STRESS CASE

If the workers' comp claim is due to stress, more questions regarding the injured worker's personal life will be necessary.

"Have you experienced any marital problems? Do you get along with your ex-spouse? Are you receiving or paying alimony? Are you receiving or paying child support? Have you had any problems with your children, drugs, finances, criminal charges, spouse employment, a decrease in pay, job stability, neighbors, or deaths in the family?"

SUBROGATION

Subrogation is defined as finding third-party liability that can be recoverable. For example, if a worker is driving a truck on the job, and he gets sideswiped, he is covered under workers' comp, but the insurance companies can go after the other driver's insurance policy. It's a way for the workers' comp insurance companies or commercial auto insurance carriers to get reimbursed for damages.

An example of subrogation is general liability, an injury received by a worker at the premises of a third party. Maybe the worker slipped and fell on a metal grate delivering packages to another company's warehouse. During questioning, investigators should be looking for subrogation opportunities by identifying third parties who might be liable.

CURRENT MEDICAL TREATMENT

At this point in the questioning, it's time to delve into the injured worker's current medical treatment, starting with the first doctor's appointment, then asking a series of questions for each subsequent doctor's appointment. Vital information includes the date of each visit, the facility, address, type of practice, reason for treatment, exams performed, tests performed, diagnoses, and any medications or devices prescribed. It's also good to ask when the next appointment will be. This same line of questioning can be replicated for every doctor the worker has visited. After that, it's time to look a little further into their medical history.

"Have you received any treatment from alternative medical providers for the injury in this claim? Have you ever injured the same body part? If a prior injury happened, when did it occur? How and where did it happen? What kind of treatment did you receive? Where did you get the treatment? Did you lose time from work? Were any claims filed? What's the status of those claims? Do you have any current complaints as a result?"

These same questions will be asked for all prior injuries of any kind, all prior illnesses, surgeries, and medical conditions. Prior injuries might have been recreational, sports related, or prior work injuries. Questions need to be asked to clarify all of these things.

"Where did you get treatment for your prior injury? Did you lose time from work? Did you ever file a claim for it? If so, what's the status? Do you have any current problems as a result? Have you ever been involved in a motor vehicle accident at any time as a driver, passenger, or even pedestrian? If so, what was the date and location? What injuries were sustained? Did you lose time from work? Was there a police report taken? Was there an insurance claim or injury claim filed? Do you have personal healthcare insurance? If so, who's the carrier? What's the name, the group number, member number, phone number, address?"

As you can see, questions about medical history must be exhaustive. A clear picture of the injured worker's medical condition must be painted in order to understand their situation and establish liability.

OUTSIDE CONTRIBUTING FACTORS

After dealing with their medical history, it's time to investigate any outside contributing factors.

"Do you use tobacco products? How often? Do you use alcohol products? How often? Did you use alcohol products on or around the date of the injury? Do you use illegal or controlled substances? Did you use illegal or controlled substances on or around the date of the injury? Do you use any over-the-counter or prescription medications? Did you use over-the-counter or prescription medications on or around the date of the injury?"

It's helpful to know what the injured worker does when they're not working to discover if anything might have contributed to the accident.

"Do you bowl, golf, knit? Who does yard work? Do you regularly participate in any athletic activities? If the injury is carpal tunnel syndrome, do you use a home computer? What are your texting habits? Are you enrolled in any type of training or educational program? Were you enrolled at the time of the accident?"

WRAPPING UP

The best practice is to cover anything that was discovered during background checks to see if the injured worker's answers during the interview line up with what the background checks revealed. At the very end of the interview, the interviewer should clarify that the interview was voluntary and recorded with the permission of the witnesses and any photographs were taken with permission. The door should be left open for follow-up questions at a later date.

With a simple injury, the interview might last an hour, but more complicated injuries can take much longer. It's safe to assume the interview will last around ninety minutes. That leaves plenty of room for thorough answers.

In California, insurance companies have ninety days to either accept or deny a claim. If they fail to make a decision within that time period, the claim is automatically accepted. Ideally, all interviews should be conducted within the first thirty days.

Apex always conducts background checks prior to an interview. This provides vital information to direct our questioning. We once interviewed a golfer who had posted his scores on the PGA website. During the interview, he claimed he didn't play golf, but we had already seen evidence to the contrary. This established a pattern of lying.

We didn't challenge him during the interview. Instead, we used that information as a clue to direct surveillance later on.

SPECIFIC GUIDELINES

All of this in-depth questioning is meant to identify clues that can help to determine liability or compensability, and if needed, help the investigation and, specifically, inform the surveillance. By probing into their military service, the injured worker might reveal that an IED damaged their calf muscle. By addressing all of their past medical problems, the injured worker might admit they have degenerative disc disease. By asking about past lawsuits, the injured worker might mention that they pursued a civil lawsuit a few years earlier in which they were awarded $15,000 for a back injury and visited a chiropractor for six months. All of this information will have a bearing on the current claim.

CASE STUDIES

Maria was a fifty-four-year-old female laborer with an injury claim for her head, neck, upper extremities, back, and shoulders. The company suspected her of omitting prior injuries to the same body parts involved in the claim. Allegedly, she sustained her injury while trying to catch a coworker who had fallen off a trailer. The claim was accepted and benefits were issued in the form of medical treatment and temporary disability payments.

Shortly after filing the claim, she claimed that her neck, pinky finger, and left shoulder were also injured. Because she was a seasonal worker, her temporary disability benefits ended when the season ended. This angered her. Even though she was a seasonal worker, she expected to receive payments indefinitely.

She hired an attorney to file, pursue, and litigate the claim. During her deposition, she testified that she had a prior workers' comp claim for a wrist injury more than ten years earlier. However, she denied having any other injuries.

She also admitted to being involved in an automobile accident twelve years earlier. When records were subpoenaed after the deposition, her prior workers' comp claim revealed that she had suffered injuries to her bilateral wrists and neck. Those records also indicated the automobile accident had injured her left shoulder, neck, back, and chin, and she had used an unknown chiropractor to treat the injuries.

These were the same body parts for which she was filing a claim. In summary, she lied under penalty of perjury, stating that she'd only injured the palm of her left hand in the motor vehicle accident when, in fact, she'd suffered far more injuries that overlapped the current injury in this particular claim.

MELISSA'S STORY

Melissa, a forty-seven-year-old bus driver, had only been on the job for three months when she filed a cumulative trauma claim for injuries to her ankle, knee, and thigh. The company suspected her of omitting information about preexisting conditions to her lower extremities during her deposition, and they also suspected the treating physicians of grossly overinflating the level of her disability. Medical records were subpoenaed from her private physician and revealed a past history of bilateral plantar fasciitis, heel pain, bilateral foot pain, diabetes, and bilateral neuropathic pain.

She had basically lied to everyone. In reality, she had made routine visits to emergency rooms and medical facilities on a nonindustrial basis up until the year she filed the claim. Originally, she demanded a settlement of $160,000, but after these records were disclosed, the settlement was reduced to $2,500.

The insurance company decided to settle with Melissa, writing her a check for $2,500. However, that didn't stop the criminal case from going forward. After all of the lies were uncovered, the district attorney in Los Angeles

County filed a criminal case, charging her for lying under oath in her deposition, a violation of California Penal Code 664-118(a), and knowingly submitting a false claim for workers' comp benefits, a violation of Penal Code 550. She had lied to the qualifying medical evaluator and the treating physicians. She was also charged for knowingly omitting information about her preexisting condition to her medical examiner, a violation of penal code 550(b)(3), and since she lied to three other doctors as well, each instance was a separate charge.

Because no claim investigation took place, nobody ever conducted surveillance or went to her house to speak with her. If an investigator had done so, he might have spotted evidence of her preexisting conditions, such as a handicap sticker on her vehicle license plate.

Early in an investigation, the investigator will start digging deep into the injured worker's medical history, which includes canvasing medical facilities in the area to discover if she's received treatment that she failed to disclose. The up-front cost of an early investigation would have been around $8,000, but it might have saved the company the $30,000 in total costs they wound up spending. Fortunately, in this case, the injured worker was caught, but that is not always the case.

CHAPTER 7

BACKGROUND CHECKS

There are many myths about background checks that continue to be widely held. Let's confront a few of the more common ones.

- **Myth:** Private investigators can run background checks on a subject and discover any and all arrests or criminal convictions.

Actually, public records for criminal convictions are not housed in one location. They're held individually in different counties, but people tend to believe they are located in some vast oracle of information somewhere. The organization that possesses the most information about criminal convictions is the FBI. Law enforcement can access FBI information, but private investigators can't. Private investigators only have access to what every public citizen has access to: public records.

Police officers use their own software, which in California is called CLETS (California Law Enforcement Telecommunication System). When an officer pulls someone over, they can access their own system to see if the individual has outstanding warrants or a criminal history. However, the system doesn't have national access to information. An officer might run a check, see that a suspect has no criminal history, and decide to let him go, not realizing that he actually has warrants in Florida.

This is a problem both in law enforcement and private investigations. We simply can't get all of the information all of the time. In seeking information, we have to look in very specific locations. For example, if the investigator knows that a suspect lived in Boston but grew up in New York, he could run a background check in the specific counties where the suspect lived to find any criminal convictions in those locations.

However, if the suspect went to Las Vegas a few years earlier and got arrested, the investigator might not know to look there. In California alone, there are forty-nine counties, and many of them still don't have electronic records. In those instances, the only way to check their records is to go in person to municipal or superior court and ask them for access.

- **Myth:** Private investigators can get criminal records simply by using the subject's Social Security number.

That is not how criminal records are held. To find information on a specific person, the investigator needs their full name and date of birth. If the suspect has a common name like Bob Smith or Jose Rodriguez, the investigator will have to sift through numerous files to locate the one person with the correct birth date. It's an extremely tedious task, and it has to be done one county at a time. There is no central database. More counties go online every year, charging a fee for access, but even then, it's still a county-by-county search.

Many third-party companies collect county information and sell the data in bulk to help insurance and investigation companies. Thomson Reuters is one such company, collecting and presenting county information in a streamlined way to law firms, investigation companies, insurance companies, and even law enforcement. However, these companies are only contracted with specific counties, so they still lack access to many locations.

Data providers have disclaimers that state their information is only a guideline. Investigators still have to individually search specific counties, because some of the data acquired through a third-party company might be incorrect. Names and birth dates might not line up correctly 100 percent of the time on their database. The only way to double-check is to look at the actual paper file at the county office. This is a time-consuming process that takes a lot of skill, patience, and hard work.

- **Myth:** Investigators can guarantee that they will find all content posted about a certain individual on social media.

Social media profiles aren't always easy to locate. Many profiles have nicknames or code names instead of actual names (e.g. "CowboyBob1" rather than "BobJones1972"). Posts are created manually, so there's never a guarantee that an investigator will be able to find all of the content posted online about an individual. To discover if someone has posted about the subject of the investigation, a full social media search is required for numerous individuals across all of their social media accounts. It's very time consuming and tedious, but there's no way around it.

Sometimes, a subject's social media profile is set to private, in which case the information simply can't be accessed. Using a ruse to gain access is considered an invasion of privacy. It might seem reasonable to simply befriend the person online in order to view their posts, but that's also an invasion of privacy. The alternative is to look at the social media profiles of their friends and family, hoping that some of them are not set to private, in order to get a peek at the subject's activity.

- **Myth:** Private investigators can confirm whether someone is operating a business.

Many businesses operate illegally or under the table, with no definite records on file. Unfortunately, investigators are limited in what they can find out. Basically, there are three options.

First, the investigator can look for any business affiliations with the injured worker. Second, they can search for fictitious business listings or filing. Third, they can search business licenses.

The Secretary of State houses all LLCs, C corps, S corps, partnerships, and other business entities in a single statewide database. This can be useful for finding any business associated with the injured worker, but the investigator must know the name of the business in order to search the database. It's not possible to simply enter the question, "Does Bob Smith have a business?"

Fictitious business name statements must be searched in each county directly and in the specific county where the business is located. This requires some guesswork. For example, if the subject lives in Las Vegas, but their business license was established in Laughlin, Nevada, the investigator might look in the wrong place without knowing it. To narrow down the possible counties, investigators start by searching in counties where the subject has lived in the past.

To make matters worse, business name statements are not required to own a business. The subject might not even possess a business license. Some cities and counties don't require one. Searching for a specific business license must be conducted directly within each city and will only give results for businesses operating within that city.

THE EVOLUTION OF BACKGROUND CHECKS

In the past, limited information was available through database background checks, though more have been added over time. For example, California and several other states now keep a record of vehicle sighting reports, which contain every license plate that appears on their camera system. Those records are available. All you have to do is enter a license plate number, and the state database will sift through all of the stored video footage to find the vehicle with that license plate, along with the specific dates, times, and locations that it appeared on camera.

(Note: The California State Legislature is debating ending this due to public pressure.)

Originally, background checks were used to verify the moral character of a subject of an investigation, but over the years, they have evolved into a more extensive investigative tool used in so many new ways. They are now a must during pre-employment.

Social media plays a role in this as well, though case law has limited what employers can do in regard to social media and background checks. Specifically, employers in California are prohibited from using social media to preclude a potential hire from getting a job. In a workers' comp investigation, both social media and background checks can be used as long as they were not accessed illegally. This information plays a key role in looking for red flags about a specific claim, but it also helps determine how surveillance will be conducted.

EDEX AND EAMS

When investigators conduct a background check, the first thing they look for are prior workers' comp claims. In California, this information comes from EAMS.

EDEX (Electronic Data Exchange System) is a service that provides prior workers' comp claims history. The standard was EDEX, but the search doesn't provide any information unless there's a Social Security number on file with a particular claim. For this reason, smart investigators always include an EAMS (Electronic Adjudication Management System) search because EAMS searches claims history by name, date of birth, and location.

If an injured worker files a claim, and he was on the job for six months before the incident, it's a good idea to run both an EDEX and EAMS search to cross-reference the injured worker's name. This will reveal if they have ever filed similar claims.

CREDIT REPORTS

Investigators can't purchase a credit report, even with the permission of the injured worker. A credit report must be purchased by an employer, landlord, loan representative, or the individual. They can be obtained from one of three major credit reporting agencies: Equifax, Experian, and TransUnion. Experian has a feature called Experian Connect, which provides an invitation to purchase their own credit report using their name, date of birth, and Social Security number. Once purchased, the person has the option of sharing the results with whomever they choose. However, this method isn't free. The individual has to pay Experian using their own credit or debit card.

MEDICAL CANVASSING

It has become quite common these days for investigators to use medical canvassing. This involves contacting every doctor, clinic, pharmacy, or treatment facility in a select area around the injured worker's home, former residence, or place of employment. This tactic has become necessary because injured workers often withhold information about prior injuries or medical visits.

> **Note:**[13] The *Standards for Privacy of Individually Identifiable Health Information* ("Privacy Rule") establishes, for the first time, a set of national standards for the protection of certain health information. The U.S. Department of Health and Human Services ("HHS") issued the Privacy Rule to implement the requirement of the Health Insurance Portability and Accountability Act of 1996 ("HIPAA"). The Privacy Rule standards address the use and disclosure of individuals' health information—called "protected health information" by organizations subject to the Privacy Rule—called "covered entities," as well as standards for individuals' privacy rights to understand and control how their health information is used. Within HHS, the Office for Civil Rights ("OCR") has responsibility for implementing and enforcing the Privacy Rule with respect to voluntary compliance activities and civil money penalties.

---

13   U.S. Department of Health & Human Services. "Summary of the HIPAA Privacy Rule." https://www.hhs.gov/hipaa/for-professionals/privacy/laws-regulations/index.html (accessed May 14, 2018)

Due to the HIPAA law (Health Insurance Portability and Accountability Act of 1996), when contacting a medical facility, an investigator can't ask about an individual's specific health problems or diagnoses. The only information they can obtain is whether or not the injured worker has visited the facility. With that information, lawyers can subpoena for more specific information.

In some cases, a worker who lacks healthcare insurance will attempt to use workers' comp as a substitute. For example, a worker might injure his ankle while playing softball over the weekend, show up to work on Monday, and claim the injury was caused while working in the warehouse. That way, he will get sent to a workers' comp doctor for diagnosis and treatment.

During medical canvassing, the investigator might learn the worker visited a clinic on Saturday after the softball game and paid fifty dollars for a leg brace. Unfortunately, neighborhood clinics aren't part of a massive, centralized database, so investigators have to contact them one by one to find out about the Saturday appointment. During the deposition, the injured worker will be questioned about this information.

"Sir, did you happen to visit any other clinics for this injury?"

"No, I did not."

"Then, can you please tell us about your appointment at ABC Clinic on the Saturday prior to your workers' compensation claim?"

FINANCIAL INFORMATION AND PRIVACY

The Graham-Leach-Bliley Act[14] (GLBA), also known as the Financial Services Modernization Act of 1999, is a federal law that protects financial privacy rights for individuals by regulating the ways in which financial institutions safeguard the private information of consumers. The act has three sections: the Financial Privacy Rule, the Safeguards Rule, and the Pretexting Rule.

The Financial Privacy Rule determines and restricts the collection and disclosure of private financial information. The Safeguards Rule requires financial institutions to implement security programs to protect financial information. Finally, the Pretexting Rule prohibits accessing private financial information using false pretenses, which protects Social Security numbers, bank account numbers, and credit history.

The Pretexting Rule is the most important part of GLBA for private investigators, because at one time, it was very common to use ruses to obtain financial information. Prior

---

14   Federal Trade Commission. "Gramm-Leach-Bliley Act." https://www.ftc.gov/tips-advice/
business-center/privacy-and-security/gramm-leach-bliley-act. (Accessed on May 8, 2018)

to GLBA, some investigator would call a bank, talk to a manager, and pretend to be the injured worker.

At one time, all anyone needed to obtain financial information was a Social Security number, date of birth, full name, and address. Now, they are subject to a whole series of security questions from the financial institution intended to confirm their identity. This level of security is required by GLBA and is designed to protect the consumer.

The GLBA also requires clear disclosure from all financial institutions of their privacy policy regarding the sharing of nonpublic personal information with both affiliates and third parties. Notice must be sent to consumers informing them of the opportunity to opt out of the sharing of nonpublic personal information with nonaffiliated third parties, subject to certain limited exceptions.

CASE STUDY

In 2011, news broke about the possible firing of Patricia Dunn, chairwoman of Hewlett-Packard. The board of directors at Hewlett-Packard is loaded with heavyweights, and one of them leaked the information to the press. Dunn wanted to figure out who had done it, so she authorized a spying operation and put it in the hands of an outside investigator who did some questionable things.

The investigator and his operatives obtained the phone records of board members, employees, and the journalists who wrote the story. They even considered entering the San Francisco office of the *Wall Street Journal* and posing as a cleaning crew in order to snoop around.

At that time, the laws about pretexting were just starting to change. To complicate matters, private data companies were located in places like Florida (which has loose privacy laws) or offshore in the Cayman Islands, Jamaica, and the British Virgin Islands, and many investigators used those providers to sell them confidential information like phone records.

The investigator would call the cell phone service provider and pretend to be the customer in order to obtain this information. By doing this for every board member, employee, and journalist, they were able to draw lines and make connections, creating a timeline to isolate the leak. When Dunn finally learned who had leaked the story to the press, she publicly fired him from the board.

Since the Hewlett-Packard board was stacked with powerful billionaires, they fought back. The board went to the FBI and the Attorney General, seeking action against Hewlett-Packard. In the end, the investigators were convicted, and Hewlett-Packard settled with the state for $14.5 million. This case ended pretexting for phone records in the U.S., including offshore loopholes.

FAIR GAME

Any information that is publicly available is fair game in an investigation. In April of 2017, Congress passed Senate Joint Resolution 34,[15] allowing cell phone and internet service providers (ISPs) to sell the data collected for marketing. Under the regulation rollback, there are a few limits on the ways ISPs are allowed to interact with sensitive user data. That includes not just allowing providers to create marketing profiles based on the browsing history of their users but also letting them deploy undetectable tools that track web traffic. This provides another way for investigators to acquire information.

Unfortunately, much of an injured worker's online information is contained in social media. We've touched on the nuances of social media already, but let's take a deeper look at which practices are permitted in gleaning information from various social media platforms during a workers' comp investigation.

---

15 Congress. "S.J.Res.34." Congress.gov. https://www.congress.gov/bill/115th-congress/senate-joint-resolution/34. (Accessed on May 8, 2018)

CHAPTER 8

SOCIAL MEDIA INVESTIGATIONS

Social media is more widespread than ever. The first platform to hit big was Myspace, though its popularity has waned. Facebook, Instagram, Twitter, Snapchat—these days, it seems like a new social media platform appears every day.

Venmo is a recent addition. It's a money transfer app owned by PayPal that is exclusive to mobile devices, but it also operates as a social media platform. If ten people go to dinner, and one person pays, the others can log into Venmo, find that person in their contacts list, and send them their share of the money for the meal. People use it to pay their friends, their landscaper, their housekeeper—just about anyone.

Interestingly, the platform is set to automatically share all information with users. If you select a Venmo user's profile, you can see all of their activity, including both the payments they've sent and the money they've received, as well as attached comments. As an investigator, we find this amount of information sharing to be quite shocking.

These days, people want to share every thought and action on social media. On Yelp, they describe and review every meal they've eaten. On Amazon, they describe and review every product they've purchased. They comment on the songs they listen to on Spotify. It never ends. This means searching social media during a background check is a more exhausting process than ever, but it also means more and more activity is available as people choose to self-surveil.

Adding to the complexity, each social media platform has its own preferred demographic. Young people no longer focus on Facebook. The average user for Facebook has gotten older. Instead, young people prefer Instagram and Snapchat. Twitter used to have more restrictions with its post length, but those restrictions have been loosened. That means posts are longer, and they often connect to other platforms and media outlets.

CONDUCTING A SOCIAL MEDIA INVESTIGATION

When an investigator conducts a social media investigation, they will check everything on the web, including around a thousand websites. That includes everything from photo-sharing sites like Photobucket, to Amazon reviews, Craigslist, Facebook, Vine, blogs, and every major social media platform.

This is a tedious process, and there is no shortcut. There's no way to look at every website and platform at the same time. Further complicating the matter, people often use aliases online. Outside of LinkedIn, users don't have to use their real names, and even if they wanted to, they often can't because no two names can be alike and there can only be one "John Smith."

Once an investigator locates a user's social media profile, they will read all of the injured worker's posts to see if what they say online lines up with what they say about their injuries on the claim form, to the treating physician, QME, AME, or in the deposition. In one instance, a worker with an orthopedic injury claim posted videos of his band on YouTube. We learned the band's schedule and conducted surveillance at a bar with their approval. There were also lots of other people recording the show on their phones, which later ended up being posted online. He was recorded during the performance acting in a manner inconsistent with his claimed injury. We verified this with his doctor, and the worker dropped his claim.

In another case, we had a worker who claimed to have injured his back on the job so severely that he could no longer walk. However, through social media posts, we determined that he had recently purchased a brand-new pair of skis. We conducted surveillance to catch him in the act of skiing.

Any public social media post is fair game. In particular, investigators look for information that can aid in surveillance or that could lead to a subpoena of records. For example, if an injured worker reveals on Instagram that she has a second job, the defense attorney can subpoena records from the second employer. If the injured worker posts about participating in activities with a friend, defense attorneys could subpoena that friend for a deposition.

Bear in mind, just because information contained in a post is damaging does not necessarily mean it's considered proof. That's why the information gleaned from social media is often used for further investigation.

THE IMPORTANCE OF METADATA

According to Merriam-Webster,[16] "Metadata is data that provides information about other data." During any investigation, the metadata—information attached to photos, videos, and blogs—must always be collected. This information typically identifies the creator, creation date, location, copyright information, and more. The metadata must be submitted in court to corroborate the information or data submitted as evidence.

In litigation, metadata typically is used to discredit or support other evidence. For example, it could prove a certain user created a Facebook post at a specific time and at a specific location or from an internet protocol (IP) address.

Simply providing a print-out of photos is not acceptable. Courts know that images and posts can be manipulated, so they want proof of where it came from and when.

Recently, the FBI announced that they had arrested someone involved in the recent presidential campaign, who deleted all his Facebook information after realizing he was under investigation. However, deleting posts doesn't necessarily eliminate the evidence. FBI investigators already had the metadata. That metadata is the proof of a post's existence, even if the user later deletes it.

---

16 Merriam-Webster. "Definition of Metadata." https://www.merriam-webster.com/dictionary/metadata (accessed May 14, 2018)

Although metadata behind videos, photos, and blogs is lengthy, it needs to be presented as evidence in court. Three or four pages worth of posts from a Facebook page might translate into sixty pages of metadata, but it all must be downloaded, saved, and printed out. This is important for all stakeholders to understand, and it's important for investigators to ensure.

It's important for investigators to ensure that metadata is downloaded live, so it is captured the minute it was created. It is preserved up to the point the account was last indexed, which we do every single day. Most metadata reports for Facebook and Instagram accounts are a few thousand pages long. The longest one we've seen was 35,000 pages.

PROHIBITED PRACTICES

Some social media investigation practices are prohibited by law. For example, case law prohibits friending people on social media by using a ruse. An investigator can't communicate with a user's social media profile, even if their profile is open to the public. Investigators can't post responses to an injured worker's posts either. Few people are aware of this because these restrictions are mostly based on recent case law.

The most essential thing to remember when searching

social media is that photos, videos, and posts are not considered evidence without the metadata. Investigators must download all metadata. Not only can this be presented as evidence, but it can be used to direct surveillance long before the claim is settled, adjudicated, or closed.

CHAPTER 9

WHEN IS SURVEILLANCE NEEDED?

To determine the proper use of surveillance, we need to clarify when surveillance should be initiated. When an injured worker files a claim, examining or adjusting the claim is the responsibility of a claims examiner, who will interview the injured worker (if the injured worker isn't represented) and any witnesses, in an attempt to understand the claim and to determine compensability, as well as administer benefits.

During that stage in the process, the claims examiner might notice red flags. Maybe the injured worker is evasive or hard to reach. Maybe they were about to be laid off when they filed the claim, or maybe there were no witnesses. We discussed many of these red flags earlier, and a comprehensive list is provided in the appendix. However, when a cluster of red flags has been identified, that's when it's time to begin an investigation.

Through surveillance, the investigator tries to capture a few days in the life of the injured worker to see if there is any inconsistency regarding their claimed injuries. According to the Fair Claims Reporting Act, it is neither ethical nor statutorily correct to surveil every investigation. People filing claims have rights. Therefore, an articulatable suspicion must first be identified.

APPROPRIATE TIMES TO USE SURVEILLANCE

When is it appropriate to use surveillance? The short answer is, when there's an articulatable suspicion of fraud—when some evidence, clue, tip, or red flag is present. It could be when an employee claims he's so badly injured that he's unable to do anything (which seems inconsistent with that type of injury), when there's a strong reason to believe the limitations of an injury are not as bad as stated, when it is learned the employee is working somewhere else, or when the claim has grown in severity since the initial report.

Sometimes, other workers are aware that a claim is fraudulent. Sometimes, an injured worker files a claim, and then a coworker goes to HR or a supervisor and gives an eyewitness account that suggests the injured worker is lying. In those instances, surveillance is the best way to find direct evidence of the lie.

Surveillance also helps when an injured worker is malingering or exaggerating. An employee might have a legitimate, verifiable accident, but the alleged injuries seem way out of proportion with the nature of the accident, or else they don't meet the medical-based evidence standard. For example, according to ACOEM guidelines,[17] an injured worker with a torn Anterior Cruciate Ligament (ACL) in the knee should be able to run on a treadmill after thirteen to sixteen weeks. What if the injured worker keeps complaining about an inability to walk or bear any weight on their knee six to eight months later, even though MRIs show no remaining damage? At this point, the pain is entirely subjective, and no evidence supports the claim, even though the initial sprain was legitimate. Surveillance can discover the true current condition of the injured worker.

When filing a claim, injured workers are required to disclose if they have any supplemental employment. Once it becomes an indemnity claim, where the injured worker

---

17 American College of Occupation and Environmental Medicine. "Knee Disorders." State of California Department of Industrial Relations. https://www.dir.ca.gov/dwc/MTUS/ACOEM_ Guidelines/Knee-Disorders-Guideline.pdf p.384. (accessed May 8, 2018)

can't return to work, but continues to get paid, then the injured worker is required to disclose any and all sources of income. If they're getting paid under the table to paint houses or do landscaping on the weekend, they must report it. If they're running a tax preparation service out of their home during select months of the year, they must report it. Surveillance can be used to confirm a suspicion about these other sources of income.

PSYCH CLAIMS

An employee may not sue his employer for stress after they've been terminated. There are several exceptions in California law:[18]

Labor Code Sec. 3208 (e)

Where the claim for compensation is filed after notice of termination of employment or layoff, including voluntary layoff, and the claim is for an injury occurring prior to the time of notice of termination or layoff, no compensation shall be paid unless the employee demonstrates by a preponderance of the evidence that actual events of employment were predominant as to all causes combined of the psychiatric injury and one or more of the following conditions exist:

---

18   California Code, Labor Code. "California Code, Labor Code - LAB § 3208.3." https://law.justia. com/codes/california/2011/lab/division-4/3200-3219/3208/. (accessed May 10, 2018)

(1) Sudden and extraordinary events of employment were the cause of the injury.

(2) The employer has notice of the psychiatric injury under Chapter 2 (commencing with Section 5400) prior to the notice of termination or layoff.

(3) The employee's medical records existing prior to notice of termination or layoff contain evidence of treatment of the psychiatric injury.

(4) Upon a finding of sexual or racial harassment by any trier of fact, whether contractual, administrative, regulatory, or judicial.

(5) Evidence that the date of injury, as specified in Section 5411 or 5412, is subsequent to the date of the notice of termination or layoff, but prior to the effective date of the termination or layoff.

There is no compensable claim against the employer for good faith personnel actions.

Labor Code Sec. 3208.3 (h)

No compensation under this division shall be paid by an employer for a psychiatric injury if the injury was substantially caused by a lawful, nondiscriminatory, good faith personnel action. The burden of proof shall rest with the party asserting the issue.

THE 51 PERCENT RULE

At least 51 percent of an injured worker's stressors must be caused from their employment.

Labor Code Sec. 3208.3 (b)(1)

In order to establish that a psychiatric injury is compensable, an employee shall demonstrate by a preponderance of the evidence that actual events of employment were predominant as to all causes combined of the psychiatric injury.

THE SIX-MONTH RULE

A worker must have at least six months on the job before he or she can file a stress claim against their employer.

Labor Code Sec. 3208.3 (d)

Notwithstanding any other provision of this division, no compensation shall be paid pursuant to this division for a psychiatric injury related to a claim against an employer unless the employee has been employed by that employer for at least six months. The six months of employment need not be continuous. This subdivision shall not apply if the psychiatric injury is caused by a sudden and extraordinary employment condition.

It's important to remember that a discrimination claim under 132a can often be added to these types of claims.

Labor Code Sec. 132a[19]

It is the declared policy of this state that there should not be discrimination against workers who are injured in the course and scope of their employment.

A claim of psychological stress often goes hand in hand with a claim for a physical injury. What began as an accepted claim for an orthopedic injury with multiple witnesses may evolve into a psych claim.

"My physical injury has started to affect my mood," the injured worker might say. "I'm depressed. I don't go anywhere. I don't do any of the things I used to do anymore."

Surveillance helps in these kinds of cases as well. Someone might claim depression or stress, but then surveillance reveals that they're having a great time, laughing, behaving normally, as well as being social.

---

19   California Legislative Information. "Labor Code." https://leginfo.legislature.ca.gov/faces/codes_displaySection.xhtml?lawCode=LAB&sectionNum=132a. (accessed May 10, 2018)

SURVEILLANCE IS A LAST LINE OF DEFENSE

Surveillance can be used during the first ninety days of the claims process, but more often, it is used after red flags have been identified later in the process.

In some cases, the early investigation produces no obvious evidence to support suspicious fraud. Neither a search of social media nor a background check reveal anything. Maybe early surveillance doesn't reveal anything either. The investigator varied the hours, but never spotted any activity in violation of restrictions. The injured worker went to the grocery store, but they only lifted grocery bags within safe limits, and they neither bent nor stooped.

Maybe the deposition has already been done, but revealed nothing of note. The investigators might even have followed the injured worker to and from the deposition to see how they behaved before and after. As the workers' compensation board hearing draws near, the injured worker demands $500,000, while the authority to settle the claim sits at $100,000.

That's a huge gap, and the insurance company's frustration comes from the fact that red flags still exist. They just couldn't catch the injured worker doing anything contradictory. With the hearing only a few weeks away, the insurance company might decide to try surveillance one last time.

During the late stages of the claims process, especially in the weeks right before the hearing, injured workers tend to become far more relaxed and comfortable. It's not uncommon to find contradictory behavior at this point.

If a year has passed since the claim was filed, and the injured worker still says he hasn't fully recovered, the surveillance at this point might discover that he has returned to his old routine: playing golf and going to the gym every day. He claims to need $500,000 because he's just as bad as he was a year ago, but evidence shows otherwise.

CONSECUTIVE DAYS

As a best practice, experts recommend conducting two or three days of surveillance consecutively. Each of those days should be eight-to-ten-hour days or more depending on the level of activity, of watching the subject involved in varied activities. If the injured worker formerly had a manufacturing job that started at six in the morning, he might get up as early as 4:00 a.m. and leave the house by 5:00 a.m. In that case, surveillance should be set up by 4:30 a.m. across the street from his house at the nearest corner. By setting up that early, neighbors are less likely to be suspicious of the new vehicle's presence.

If the investigator is in an SUV, he should be sitting in the back. Even in a car with deeply tinted windows, the back seat is still the best option. After at least two days of being in that location, if no relevant activity has taken place, it's time to vary the hours: start at noon and stay until 8:00 p.m., for example.

The vantage point needs to provide a clear view of the front door and garage as well as all of the major exits out of the neighborhood. In a rural area, finding a good vantage point or parking spot might be challenging, especially when there are no fences and the landscape is wide open and flat. Google Earth is a great tool for checking out the surrounding area beforehand.

It's a good practice to call the local police and let them know an investigator is in the neighborhood, in case a neighbor notices the suspicious vehicle and calls it in. If a police officer shows up to question the investigator, it can reveal the surveillance to the subject.

Investigators should make note of all pertinent information, even if there's no activity: types of vehicles, license plates, the condition of the landscaping. Were the lights on? Were newspapers collected at the front door? What time does the mailman come every day?

In some instances, it's simply not possible to get a clear view of the front door, in which case, the next best option is to set up surveillance at the nearest intersection, trying to catch the person as they leave the area. This might be necessary in a neighborhood where the HOA doesn't allow parking on the street, or when trying to surveil an urban high-rise apartment where the parking spaces don't match the apartment numbers. If the injured worker has children, investigators need to find out where the nearest schools are prior to conducting surveillance, so they have an idea of the route the injured worker will take.

There are instances when surveillance with one investigator proves impossible. For example, the injured worker might live in a high-rise with no public access to the building and a secured parking garage. One investigator can sit outside the garage to identify the driver, while another investigator watches the front door of the building.

If the worker's home address is unknown, conduct surveillance at their next doctor's appointment and follow them home.

MOBILE SURVEILLANCE

When an injured worker is on the move, it's time for surveillance to go mobile. Mobile surveillance is an art, and it takes time to get good at it. Before the investigator arrives onsite, they should take note of all departure routes. While mobile, investigators should drive in the injured worker's blind spot, so they don't appear in the rearview mirror constantly. Careful driving in the slow lane can prevent missing a lane change or sudden exit.

Depending on the time of day, the investigator should always allow one vehicle between the injured worker's vehicle and their own vehicle. In the morning, traffic can be heavy, so it might be necessary to follow a little closer.

In all of this, the investigator must constantly look ahead and try to anticipate where the injured worker is going. If an approaching traffic light has been green for a while, it's best to get closer to the injured worker before it turns red. At a red light, if there's no cover, the investigator can pull to the side and wait for more vehicles.

If visual contact is lost, the investigator will need to check nearby shopping centers, retail businesses, gas stations, and restaurants. If the injured worker doesn't turn up, the best option is to return to their residence and see if they've gone home. Failing that, a grid search can be attempted. This involves driving up and down every street in a six to ten block radius, driving first along the X-axis and then along the Y-axis.

GETTING BURNED

When an investigator's position is compromised, that's what is known in the industry as "getting burned." It happens to every investigator at some point. However, a few things can reduce the risks and associated problems.

Though investigators should always contact law enforcement to let them know an investigation is being conducted in the area, they should never tell the police which specific person they are watching. This is especially true in a small town, neighborhood, or community, where most of the people know each other. We experienced an incident where a person in dispatch knew the injured worker and tipped him off.

A few things make the investigator more obvious and easy to notice. Parking in the same location for two or three days starts to look suspicious. Moving the vehicle each day reduces that risk. A best practice is not to drive with daytime running lamps on and not running the engine in order to use the air conditioning.

During mobile surveillance, when the worker makes a bunch of unusual turns—U-turns in driveways, illegal U-turns in a business district—it may be a sign they've grown suspicious. If that happens, it's time to terminate surveillance for the day.

When an investigator gets burned, they must *never* reveal their identity to the injured worker. In fact, an investigator should never speak to the injured worker under any circumstances. If the injured worker starts driving in an evasive manner, it's best to let them go. Otherwise, the investigator runs the risk of being accused of stalking or harassment—and it's unsafe.

WHY IS SURVEILLANCE SO COSTLY?

Experienced claims professionals don't try to save money by, for example, limiting surveillance to four-hour time slots, because a half-hearted investigation won't net much in the way of results. Surveillance is like deep-sea fishing. When you're deep-sea fishing, you throw the line in and leave it there. The line doesn't come out of the water very often. If you treat surveillance like fly-fishing, you won't catch many fish.

There's usually a gap between the settlement demand the injured worker asks for and the amount the insurance company is willing to pay. Both sides make their arguments during negotiations or at a hearing. The injured worker's lawyer is going to push toward long-term or permanent impairment. If the lawyer succeeds, the injured worker might wind up with a settlement far larger than what they originally asked for.

Of course, the insurance company's defense lawyer is going to push the other way, arguing that the injury is not as severe, or the restrictions as stringent, as the worker claims. When video evidence from surveillance is introduced, it might not appear to be a slam dunk. However, it doesn't always need to be. The video evidence only needs to show enough to suggest the injured worker's condition is not quite as bad as claimed.

"This video was shot two weeks ago," the insurance company lawyer might say. "It clearly suggests that you're a lot better off than what you've been saying. You showed up to the hearing today with a limp, but on the video from two weeks ago, you weren't limping at all."

The injured worker's lawyer might argue, "Well, he was feeling pretty good on the day of the video. You're taking it out of context. You should have seen him an hour later, when he was on Vicodin and lying in bed."

However, even with this argument, the worker's lawyer recognizes this new obstacle in his case. In the end, the amount the insurance company settles for will be far less than what the injured worker demanded. Ultimately, that's one of the goals of surveillance, to save the insurance company money and make sure they're only paying a fair amount for legitimate claims.

If the original demand was $500,000, but the worker settled for $180,000, that's a $320,000 cost savings. By comparison, two or three days of surveillance costs under

$3,000. That might sound expensive when considered by itself, but when put into perspective, compared to the amount saved in the settlement, the benefits are clear.

Spending $3,000 to save $320,000 is a no-brainer. The Coalition Against Insurance Fraud reveals the average ROI on surveillance is in the tens of thousands, so it's a last line of defense that is well worth the cost.

A CLEARER PICTURE OF INDEMNITY RESERVES

The money that goes to the injured worker is only one part of the overall expense. The insurance company also pays the doctors, the lawyer, any transportation fees (to get the injured worker to appointments), possibly a translator, and the cost of administering the claim. All that money must be set aside in the indemnity reserves and paid out during and after the claim.

Insurance companies have to constantly monitor that reserve fund to ensure there's enough money to administer benefits. All of this is regulated by the Department of Insurance. The purpose is to prevent an insurance company from declaring bankruptcy or being insolvent and leaving the injured worker out on a limb by failing to reserve enough money for their claims.

That money must be set aside in advance and constantly

updated. The first day that a claim comes in, the money must be reserved. If a worker breaks his arm on a conveyor belt, the claims examiner has to work out the right amount to reserve.

"This is a broken left arm. Based on the compensation that would normally be paid for a permanent impairment of someone who lost the use of their left arm, we need to set aside $48,000. Doctor bills and surgeries will add another $25,000, so I'll place a total of $85,000 in reserve right away."

This must occur on day one. Over time, as other information comes in, the reserves can go up or down. The reserve might start at $85,000, but then the injured worker is rushed to the hospital for emergency surgery. Suddenly, the situation has worsened, and now the reserves climb to $150,000 because the company knows this worker will not be back on the job anytime soon. Maybe it becomes clear as the weeks pass that the damage is more severe than initially thought. The arm is never going to be the same, which means they will receive compensation for a permanent impairment.

Claims examiners and insurance companies are sensitive to the reserves going up because, after all, companies have to remain solvent. When reserves are high, it eats into the general fund. If the settlement ends up being more than the reserves, the insurance company is facing a major loss. In the end, premiums to the insurance company will have to rise in order make up the difference.

An investigation company helps by providing a clearer picture of whether or not the worker's injury and behavior are consistent. This, in turn, helps insurance companies set their reserves at a more accurate level. For example, if a worker puts in a claim for a back injury, and surveillance shows that they wear a back brace and use a motorized cart wherever they go, that they never lift anything or bend over, then it strengthens their claim. The insurance adjuster can say, "The worker told a confused story during the deposition, and they were in a car accident last year, but the severity of their claim seems to be legitimate. We have to increase the reserves." This, at least, ensures that enough money will be set aside to cover the settlement.

LOSS ADJUSTMENT EXPENSES

In 2015, the Workers' Comp Insurance Rating Bureau (WCIRB) conducted a State of the System report using numbers from 2014. They determined that the estimated average medical cost per indemnity claim in California was $43,750, and that only includes medical benefits, not permanent impairment costs.

In addition to the indemnity and medical benefits, insurers

incur expenses related to the handling and administration of workers' compensation claims. Those expenses, known as loss adjustment expenses, include the cost of the insurance claims staff to administer the claims, the cost of the attorneys and other legal expenses in defending claims, medical costs, containment programs, and other court and claim-related expenses. The average loss adjustment cost per indemnity claim in 2014 was $13,000.

California indemnity costs per claim are well above the median level. To a large extent, the above-average indemnity costs in the state are driven by the high number of claims involving permanent impairment benefits, which average $26,446 per claim. All combined, the average claim in California, including indemnity, permanent impairment, medical costs, and claim handling, comes to an average of $86,000.

The number of permanent impairment claims in California is among the highest in the nation, with Los Angeles driving claims frequency. Medical costs in California are also among the highest in the nation, but recent declines suggest that things are trending in the right direction. Oddly, indemnity costs are reported and settled much slower in California than in other states. That's a problem because the longer these claims go on, the more expensive they become.

Surveillance can be used to cut the time of settlement

drastically. For example, if a doctor believes the injured worker's complaint that they are improving slowly, the investigator can show the doctor surveillance that proves the injured worker is doing better than they say. The doctor, in turn, can stop or drastically reduce treatment time, potentially shaving off months or years from the claims process.

OTHER BEST PRACTICES FOR SURVEILLANCE

All of an investigator's equipment, including vehicles, must be in good working condition. A dead battery in the middle of surveillance can be incredibly frustrating. A full tank of gas and clean windows are also important.

Of course, the investigator needs to make sure they're following the right person. We know of one instance where the investigator spent hours videotaping the wrong person. He ran the license through the DMV, and the DMV came back with the right name. The person driving the vehicle fit the physical description.

In the end, the investigator followed this person for three days and captured a lot of great video footage. Six months later, during the hearing, when the injured worker saw the footage, he said, "That's not me." As it turned out, he had an identical twin brother. That made all of the video footage useless.

Having multiple clear images of the injured worker helps ensure the right person is being surveilled. Fortunately, these days, more employers are taking photographs during the employment process, and some require photos for security purposes to get in and out of the building. Another good source of photos is social media.

Another best practice is to make sure the date and time stamp is accurate on any video footage. Investigators should never alter this after the footage has been recorded, since that could be considered tampering with evidence.

As mentioned in a previous chapter, all video needs to be taken in public areas or on private property with verified permission. California law expressly allows pretexting when an investigator is looking into allegations of insurance fraud, but it has to be done in a way that doesn't violate privacy. If the gates of the community are wide open for a neighborhood garage sale, and a big sign says, "Everyone Welcome," that's an open invitation.

AVOIDING PITFALLS

It is critical to maintain the chain of evidence. The investigator must be able to prove a continuity of possession and security of all original copies of any video surveillance, whether it's a physical or digital copy.

A physical copy needs documentation showing that it remained in the possession of the investigator until it was personally handed over as evidence. Just like evidence held by law enforcement, copies can be distributed, but the original must remain in locked storage. During a hearing, when the original is presented, a clear chain of possession prevents the worker's lawyer from arguing the footage was potentially tampered with.

The entire video is always required. Key footage is enough to give a quick snapshot to doctors and often judges, because they don't always have time to view all of the video during a hearing. A claims professional doesn't want to watch hours of video either. A condensed version gets the point across. However, a summary of the entire video along with the original copy must be brought to the hearing.

Video must be shown in sequence. Day two shouldn't be presented before day one. Video clips must never be moved around or shown in the wrong order. An improper sequence makes people suspect the footage was manipulated or edited.

Remember, best practices don't apply only to surveillance or the investigator. For the best possible outcome, best practices should be implemented by everyone involved in the workers' compensation claim process. In the next chapter, we'll take a more comprehensive look at best practices and how they apply across the board.

CHAPTER 10

BEST PRACTICES

Best practices mean making sure that every "T" is crossed and every "I" is dotted from the very beginning of a claim, especially as it relates to accepting or denying a claim, and determining if an investigation needs to occur. If claims aren't handled properly right out of the gate, it will be harder to determine if there's fraud or the potential for malingering. It might be months into the process before red flags become clear.

When you keep the barn door closed, the horses stay inside. A few might get out every once in a while. In the same way, best practices at the very beginning prevent most fraudulent claims from getting through. According to the Coalition on Insurance Fraud, once an injured worker obtains legal representation, the average claim cost increases by 40 percent or more.

A small, unsophisticated employer may not have rigid protocols in place for dealing with workers' comp claims. Under fifty employees, they probably aren't big enough to have an HR department that is trained in workers' comp. Typically, this isn't a problem, because a small company doesn't get many claims annually.

At the same time, that company is probably unfamiliar with the risks, dangers, and red flags. Suddenly, this unsuspecting employer gets hit with a workers' comp claim, and they don't know how to respond. They don't know to stop everything, take pictures, talk to coworkers, and talk to other employees and supervisors to find out what happened. They don't know how important it is to get the full story right away.

An unsophisticated employer can overlook major red flags and fail to report them to the insurance company. Since the insurance company doesn't know about the red flags, they approve the claim, and things quickly spiral out of control. By the time red flags occur later in the process, the injured worker is already getting paid to stay at home while racking up medical bills.

Prevention is the less expensive option for businesses of every size. A company that does high-risk work, like a roofing company, can't afford to not take proper precautions. Even a large company in a safe industry with relatively few claims annually can save a lot of money by simply putting best practices into place.

A Silicon Valley company might have $100 million in annual sales and 500 employees, but because of the nature of their work, they will rarely get a workers' comp claim. However, when they do, it's probably an unfamiliar process to them, and they might not understand how to deal with it. Unfortunately, their impressive sales and unfamiliarity with workers' comp make them a tempting target for someone wanting to take advantage of the system. No matter how big the company is, if they have a low claims volume, they can make the same mistakes as a small, unsophisticated company.

Whether large or small, every company should institute the formal protocols mandated, legislated, and/or required by insurance companies. That means employees must report any injury within twenty-four hours of acknowledgment of an accident, and the employer needs to send the first report about the injury to a third-party administrator or insurance company as soon as possible.

Companies can't afford to waste time. As soon as the accident occurs, the clock starts ticking on who can accept or deny the claim, who can collect evidence and eyewitness testimony, and who can control medical treatment. Time is of the essence.

BEST PRACTICES FOR CLAIMS EXAMINERS

For claims examiners, a good practice is to avoid litigation because it adds costs to the claim. The best way to avoid litigation is by acting fairly in the administration of a claim. When the worker needs treatment, approve and authorize the necessary treatment promptly. Workers often seek litigation because they feel they aren't being treated fairly or their claim isn't getting attention.

For claims with numerous red flags, the worker is likely to hire a lawyer anyway. In fact, hiring a lawyer immediately is a good sign the worker has been through the workers' comp process before. It's possible that they know their side of the story doesn't add up, or they're trying to avoid answering questions directly, so they need a lawyer to do the talking for them.

Even a legitimate claim can turn into a malingering case if the worker feels like they're being mistreated. They start to think, "The company doesn't care about me. I worked hard and hurt my back, and they don't want to help me. I'll show them. I'm getting a lawyer." Remember the elements of fraud.

In one case we know about, a certain city that lacked the funds to hire their own sanitation workers outsourced the work to a private, garbage collection company. One day, early in the morning, an eighty-six-year-old woman stepped outside just as the garbage truck pulled up in front of her house. She had forgotten to dump a small waste basket, so she carried it to the garbage can and opened the lid.

What she didn't realize is the truck already had another garbage can gripped in its electronic arm. Since the driver didn't see the woman come out of her house, he lowered the arm and drove the garbage can right on top of her head.

An accident of that sort would have injured anyone, but because of the woman's age, she suffered a severe injury. She was rushed to the hospital in critical condition. The first thing the company did was send an investigator to find out exactly what happened.

Within twenty-four hours, evidence had been secured and all witnesses had been interviewed. At the same time, the company made sure the injured woman was taken care of. They apologized for what happened and offered their full support. The woman and her family saw the company take ownership of the problem and bear responsibility throughout her recovery. As a result, when she finally recovered, they opted not to sue.

The company's attitude was the right one: "If we take care of this injured person, do the right thing by her from the very beginning, we might not have to worry about litigation."

That's exactly what happened. Taking responsibility and treating people decently go a long way toward preventing litigation. In a case as severe as this one, a jury might easily have awarded the woman a million dollars or more in punitive damages.

VET CLAIMS BEFORE THEY START

Another best practice for claims examiners is to run a background check at the outset of the claim, especially if the examiner has noticed a red flag. In one instance, an employer failing to share the details of a claim with the insurance company early on almost had disastrous consequences.

The worker was a sign language teacher, and she developed bilateral carpal tunnel syndrome, as well as shoulder and neck problems. At first, it seems like a straightforward case. No one questioned it. She taught sign language for hours every day, so developing these particular symptoms made sense. She received treatment right away. Her doctor recommended surgery, and the school approved the surgery.

Apex was brought on board during the deposition, as the

woman was recovering from surgery. Instead of a standard insurance policy, the school was part of a self-insurance pool. A number of schools put money into the pool to pay each other's claims.

At this point, the cost of surgery, plus time off work, and other medical treatment had climbed to $130,000, but the teacher claimed she needed another $200,000 because she was permanently unable to perform sign language.

Only later did we learn from the school that she'd only been on the job for seven months, and it was her first sign language job. Her previous job had nothing to do with sign language, but she'd raised and taught her grandchild sign language from the time they were a toddler. That meant she'd been using sign language for decades prior to starting her teaching job.

On top of that, she'd had a previous neck and shoulder injury while working at another company. She hadn't disclosed that information during the hiring process, and no one thought to dig deeper into her background prior to the deposition.

When it came time to settle the claim, the school and the AME, armed with this new information, were able to argue that her cumulative trauma injury occurred before she worked for them. Though her current position may have exacerbated the injuries, they weren't the primary cause. They argued apportionment should apply, thereby reducing their exposure.

As a result, they settled for a much smaller amount than the $180,000 she requested. However, they were unable to recoup their medical costs. Had they possessed all information at the beginning of the process, they could have denied her treatment and deposed her in such a way that she was caught lying.

BEST PRACTICES FOR INVESTIGATORS

The laws regarding investigations change fast. Drone laws, which we discussed in an earlier chapter, are a good example of this.

Regarding privacy, there are federal laws, state laws, and city and local laws. An investigator might do something that is legal in the state of California but violates federal law. On top of that, case law impacts how investigations are conducted.

Case law has set precedents about using ladders to look over fences, climbing trees, peering into private backyards, cutting holes in fences, and sticking cameras over fences. All of these things are now considered trespassing.

An investigator's right to access public property is strongest when that property has historically been open to the public for the exercise of speech, public debate, and assembly. These areas, known as public forums, include sidewalks, parks, and town squares. Any public space where a person may freely enter and gather information is acceptable, but this must be done without disturbing the peace or interfering with others. The right to access a public forum does not confer immunity from all liability regarding disruptive or harassing conduct.

Investigators are allowed to videotape in such places, however the particulars are sometimes murky. For example, regarding public schools and universities, investigators have far more restrictions, due to mass shootings. Even though the investigator might be on a public university campus, they can be charged with trespassing if they lack official permission to be there.

In some cases, specific locations on a university campus are considered public forums. Buildings might be off-limits, but the quad in the center of campus might be open to the general public. Some schools make specific rooms available to the public.

An investigator cannot gather information on government-owned property that is not open to the general public. The following are examples of nonpublic forums:

- Airport terminals.

In the case *International Society for Krishna Consciousness v. Lee* in 1992, the Supreme Court declared that airports are, "Among those publicly owned facilities that could be closed to all except those who have legitimate businesses there."

- Government-owned civic centers, stadiums, or theaters used for private, commercial purposes.

When the government leases a convention center, a private lessee may legally exclude individuals who want to report on newsworthy events or investigators. The event coordinators may even grant exclusive media coverage rights to a particular media outlet and deny access to others. In those instances, permission has to be granted to go on private property.

ALWAYS OBTAIN SIGNED RELEASES

At the onset of the claims process, it's a standard business practice to request signed authorizations from injured workers to release certain types of information. Medical information is the top priority, but other important information often gets overlooked.

In a signed release, if it's in compliance with HIPAA, a

best practice is to have the injured worker sign a comprehensive, detailed release. Beyond medical information, this could include educational history or military service, as well as things like gym membership.

Another best practice is to have the injured worker fill out a body pain form. This form allows the worker to mark the location of their injuries and associated pain levels on a silhouette of a human body. They sign and date the form, and it provides a benchmark that shows how they felt at a particular moment in time.

Why is this important? If, on day one, the worker says they had a lower back injury and marked it on the form, but weeks later they claim to also have a knee injury, the body pain form can be used to contradict the new claim. Unfortunately, this happens all too often. Injured workers trying to take advantage of the system will add new injuries as a claim process progresses. It's known in the industry as "injury creep," and it's more likely to happen once a lawyer gets involved. After all, lawyers are smart enough to know that the more money they can attribute to a claim, the more money they get paid at the end.

BEST PRACTICES FOR EMPLOYERS

Employers should document all injuries that happen outside of work. If some of the employees play in a softball league, and one of them comes to work the day after a game with a pronounced limp, this needs to be documented. The employer should pull that worker aside and speak with him.

"Hey Bob, what happened to you?"

"I twisted my ankle playing softball last night."

That injury should be documented and filed with HR. If the worker ever files a claim for an injury to the same body part, the file can be pulled. It's possible the previous injury fully healed and had nothing to do with the workplace injury. On the other hand, if the employer knows about the previous injury, they can look into it during the early stages of the claim process. Maybe they will discover that the previous injury was more severe than they realized.

HUMAN RESOURCES CAN HELP REDUCE CLAIMS

Unfortunately, injured workers often complain that they told their supervisor about an injury and were ignored. It's not uncommon for an injured worker to say something like this during the investigation: "I told my supervisor two months ago that my back was bothering me, and he didn't think it was a big deal. I never got treatment, and now it's gotten so bad, I can't go to work."

In many cases, the worker is telling the truth. Too often, supervisors will hear about an injury and shrug it off. They fail to report it, which means they lose the opportunity to get on top of a possible claim.

When supervisors drag their feet, the company loses precious time to gather facts about the injury. When employers fail to take control of the aftermath of an injury, they lose control of the decision making.

"I told them in April my back was hurt," a worker might say. "I even took a couple days off, using PTO, but it's gotten worse. I saw my personal doctor, but my boss never told me to file a claim or gave me any paperwork."

Human resources, supervisors, and managers can do a lot to prevent claims from spiraling out of control by simply getting on top of them at the very beginning. The HR department must train its staff on how to handle workers' comp claims, and supervisors must be ready to respond to any injury by taking it seriously.

At one time, it was a common practice to pay a bonus to employees, managers, and executives if they didn't have any workers' comp claims for a period of time. This was a common practice in industries with high insurance premiums, like construction. That practice has become illegal because it encourages managers to tell workers, "Don't file a claim. Just get treatment outside of work. We'll pay for it." Technically, that is a form of workers' comp fraud.

BEST PRACTICES FOR LAYOFFS AND TERMINATION

As we've pointed out, fraudulent claims are more likely when people know their jobs are about to be terminated. If the company is going to have a round of layoffs, the best practice is to do it suddenly. Dragging out layoffs intensifies the stress and gives disgruntled employees ample time to set up a fraudulent claim. It tells employees, "You have thirty days to come up with an injury."

Although it sounds cutthroat, many employers have decided that it is far less risky to call a meeting on Friday afternoon at 4:30 p.m. and announce, "Unfortunately, we're having layoffs. You will receive two weeks' pay, but today is the last day of work." That eliminates the opportunity for workers to fabricate an injury on the job. Some employers, especially those sensitive to negative publicity may choose to give a longer notice period, but they, too, must be vigilant about managing potential fraudulent claims.

When a plant announces that they are closing in six months, suddenly there's a spike in workers' comp claims. This happens all too often. The more notice workers receive, the more claims for injuries will be filed.

Some post-termination claims are legitimate. A firefighter might retire and then learn they have lung cancer from breathing smoke and chemicals for years on the job. Likewise, a police officer might retire and then have a heart attack as a result of all the years of stress on the job.

On the other hand, some post-termination claims are retaliation against the company. A person gets fired, or quits, and suddenly they start complaining about back pain. The best practice for employers is to do what they can to prevent such claims from being filed in the first place. There are a few ways to do this. First, the company can offer annual physical exams and make them mandatory. Some trucking companies and the FAA, for example, already do this. That way, they can refer back to the latest exam if a worker suddenly claims cumulative trauma after getting terminated.

Some employers require exit interviews that can flush out any future claims. Another way to prevent post-termination claims is by providing severance with a full waiver of any claims. Depending on the state, that full waiver will vary in terms of what claims can be waived. Essentially, in exchange for a severance package, they would voluntarily waive the right to file any lawsuits or claims. Paying a severance may be a cost-saving measure because it can reduce the number of claims and the amount of litigation. Again, each state has its own laws that address severance and which rights can be waived.

When terminating an employee, it's a good idea to do it in a location where they can't fabricate a last-minute injury. Make sure they don't slip and fall on their way out the door or, worse yet, have a violent episode. When experienced and well-trained companies terminate employees, they do it toward the end of the day, and they clear out the worker's desk or locker beforehand. The announcement is made in a location where there's an easy exit, not in the middle of the office or factory floor. A best practice is to pack up all personal belongings and have everything ready by an exit door.

The recent trend is for claims to follow the flow of unemployment rates. In California, claims have continued to decline, even as claim costs rise. Partly, this has to do with a lower unemployment rate, fewer manual labor jobs, automation, advances in ergonomics, workplace safety, as well as the implementation of evidence-based medicine. Investigations are just another tool for employers, insurance companies, and claims professionals to use in an attempt to reduce fraud.

CONCLUSION

The laws regarding workers' comp claims and investigations are constantly changing. In order to be effective, you have to stay current with case law. When both legislation and case law change, injured workers and their lawyers can use the confusion to their advantage.

Privacy and pretexting laws began to change after Princess Diana died, as an attempt to rein in paparazzi. Lawyers have figured out many ways to apply the extra protections to insurance claims investigations. As we move into the digital age, these protections continue to get stricter, both at the federal and state level. Employers, HR professionals, risk managers, and investigators need to stay on top of the changes and anticipate that workers and their lawyers will try to use them to their advantage.

A significant motivating factor in these constant changes to privacy laws is a desire on the part of lawmakers to keep up with advances in technology. We see this most clearly in the recent drone laws, which have caused trouble for investigators. A company might approach an investigation company and ask them, "Can you fly a drone over this hill and get video of the injured worker on their rural property?" At one time, that would have been fine, but recent changes in the law have restricted drone use significantly.

If the investigator agrees to use a drone to capture the footage and the video gets introduced as evidence, one should assume it's going to cause a problem. The lawyer for the injured worker will most likely be current on all relevant case law. When he learns about the drone footage, he will likely protest, "You have violated the privacy rights of my client. This video is inadmissible, and you can be sanctioned for recording it. We're going to file a civil suit against the investigation company, the insurance company, and the employer."

Stay aware of the evolving landscape of privacy laws and implement best practices so you're ready to deal with any significant changes. It has always been a best practice for doctors to ask injured workers to fill out a body diagram chart, showing where the injury is located and what pain level is associated with it. However, doctors don't do this on every visit. Adding this step anytime they have a face-to-face interaction with an injured worker creates a series of benchmarks that can be used to measure improvement and consistency. This sends the message that the employer and insurance company are meticulous and won't be fooled by fraudulent claims, which can discourage such attempts.

To reduce the overall cost of a claim, always administer them fairly. Identify and address malingering or fraud quickly, ideally at the outset, and investigate any suspicious claims in a thorough and timely fashion to reduce and mitigate risk.

Put in place all of the best practices mentioned in this book and read through the list of red flags in the appendix. Make sure the individual administering the claim or their supervisor use the same set of best practices, so everyone is working together. With consistent effort and a thorough approach, you can reduce litigation and fraudulent claims, which will save money, keep premiums from rising, and help injured workers get the fair settlements they deserve.

APPENDIX

RED FLAGS

The following are red flags that might come up at some point during the claims process, particularly the deposition, background check, and social media check. When a cluster of red flags appear, it's time to open a surveillance investigation.

- The injury occurs on a Monday.
- The applicant is a new hire.
- The applicant took unexplained or excessive time off prior to the claimed injury.
- The applicant's alleged injury occurred prior to or just after a strike, layoff, plant closure, termination, notice of employer relocation, or completion of seasonal or temporary work.

- The applicant reported an injury immediately following a disciplinary action: probation, demotion, or being passed over for promotion.
- The applicant has a history of personal injury or workers' compensation claims.
- The applicant's job history shows many jobs held for fairly short periods of time.
- The applicant's alleged injury relates to a preexisting injury or health problem.
- The applicant uses the addresses of friends, family, or post office boxes and has no known permanent address.
- The applicant's family members have no knowledge of the injury, or, conversely, they are very knowledgeable of the injury.
- The applicant was experiencing financial difficulties or domestic problems prior to the submission of a claim.
- The applicant has high-risk activities as a hobby, such as skydiving or bungee jumping.
- The applicant's version of the accident has inconsistencies or isn't credible.
- There are no witnesses to the accident, or the witnesses to the accident tell stories that conflict with the applicant's version of the story.
- The applicant failed to report the injury in a timely manner.
- The accident or type of injury is unusual for the applicant's line of work.

- Facts regarding the accident differ in various medical reports, statements, and the employer's first report of the injury.
- The Social Security number provided does not belong to the applicant.
- The applicant refuses to produce solid or correct identification.
- The applicant avoids using the postal service, preferring to hand deliver documents.
- The applicant cannot be reached at home during work hours, although they claim to be unable to work.
- When other people at the applicant's home answer the phone, they give vague answers to the person's whereabouts.
- The applicant tends to be unavailable and elusive.
- The applicant's lifestyle does not coincide with their known income.
- Several of the applicant's family members are receiving workers' compensation, unemployment, social security, or welfare.
- The proposed long-term disability payments meet or exceed their wages after taxes.
- The applicant refuses diagnostic procedures to confirm the injury or refuses to attend a scheduled medical exam.
- The applicant's coworkers express the opinion that the injury is not legitimate.
- The alleged injuries are all subjective (e.g., soft tissue pain and emotional injuries).

- The applicant changes their version of the accident after learning of inconsistencies, misrepresentation, or fabrication by any party.
- The applicant frequently changes physicians or does so after being released to return to work.
- The physical description of the applicant indicates a muscular, well-tanned individual with calloused hands, grease under the fingernails, or other signs of active work.
- Medical treatment is inconsistent with the injuries originally alleged by the applicant.
- The applicant undergoes excessive treatment for soft tissue injuries.
- Treatment as reported by the applicant is different from the doctor's treatment in the medical report.
- The applicant is examined by several doctors.
- The applicant reports seeing a doctor for a brief period of time; however, reports and billing indicate a lengthy visit.
- Medical reports from treatment appear to be altered or are sent in by nonmedical personnel.
- The applicant lives far from the medical facility, yet receives frequent treatment there.
- Surveillance shows the applicant's activities are inconsistent with the physical limitations related to the medical reports and deposition.
- Surveillance or a tip reveals the fully disabled worker is employed elsewhere.

- The applicant cannot describe either diagnostic tests or treatment for which the employer was billed.
- The doctor ordered diagnostic testing that is not necessary to determine the extent of the applicant's injuries.
- Diagnostic tests are performed, but there is no request by a doctor in the medical files.
- Diagnostic tests are performed by a vendor not in close proximity to the doctor's office or the applicant's home.
- The vendor uses a post office box on all documents or cannot supply diagnostic records.
- The doctor or medical clinic has ownership in a diagnostic group.
- Various reports by a doctor in different applicants' cases read identically or similarly.
- A post office box is used for the clinic or doctor's address instead of a street address.
- Medical reports appear to be photocopied.
- The physician cannot be located at the address shown on documentation.
- The doctor's report never identifies the injured worker by gender or gets the gender wrong.
- New or additional medical problems are alleged and attributed to the original injury.
- Specific soft tissue injury develops into psychiatric trauma.
- The medical reports contain inaccurate terminology, spelling errors, or they are rubber stamped with a doctor's name.

- The medical facility uses multiple names or changes their name often.
- Current procedural terminology codes show evidence of an upgraded level of services.
- Bills are received for unnecessary services.
- The medical facility has consistently billed workers' comp, auto, health, or other insurance carriers and has received payments for them.
- The applicant is unable to define medical ailments as listed on the claim form.
- The lawyer's letter of representation or the letter from the medical clinic is the first notice of the claim, which means the worker didn't file the claim.
- The first time the employer heard about the claim was from a lawyer or doctor.
- The lawyer's letter is dated the same day as the reported incident or shortly thereafter.
- There's a repeated pattern of attorney referrals to the same doctor.
- The applicant states that a "friend" provided a reference to the attorney or clinic, but they can't remember the friend's name.
- The applicant alleges the doctor or clinic was found through a hotline.
- The applicant filed for unemployment or disability benefits before visiting the attorney or clinic.
- The applicant is overly pushy, demanding a quick settlement, commitment, or decision.

- The applicant is unusually familiar with the claim's handling procedures and workers' compensation process.
- Social media profiles indicate various, inconsistent statuses.

PURSUING RED FLAGS

Red flags do not automatically indicate guilt, but they are indicators of potential fraud. They need to be followed up, and when appropriate, the Special Investigations Unit or an outside organization should be consulted.

Remember what it takes to prove criminal fraud, and always ask yourselves these questions when you suspect fraud:

- What was the lie?
- Was the lie material to getting benefits?
- Was it knowingly or intentionally made?
- Was it made for the purposes of either obtaining or denying benefits?

ABOUT THE AUTHOR

 **JR ROBLES** is a former fraud investigator for the State of California. He is the CEO of Apex Investigation, a leading provider of investigative services for workers' compensation insurance professionals. After years of direct investigative experience, JR now manages daily operations and writes white papers to remain current on all applicable workers' comp laws. In this book, he shares his experience and knowledge, providing claims examiners, HR managers, and others the information they need reduce the risks and costs of workers' comp claims and mitigate fraud claims.

Made in the USA
Columbia, SC
09 July 2018